Business Rules
Management and Execution

Foreword by
Ronald G. Ross

Published in collaboration with

The Official Publication of the Business Rules Community

Future Strategies Inc., Book Division
Lighthouse Point, Florida

Business Rules:

Management and Execution

Copyright © 2020 by Future Strategies Inc.

ISBN-13: 978-0-9863214-8-1

Published by Future Strategies Inc., Book Division

Lighthouse Point FL 33064 USA
1.954.482.0693 fax 1.954.719.3746
www.FutStrat.com; www.BPM-Books.com; books@FutStrat.com

Publisher's Cataloging-in-Publication Data

© **ISBN-13: 978-0-9863214-8-1**

Business Rules: Management and Execution

/Fischer, Layna (editor)

/Ross, Ronald G; Lam, Gladys; Seer, Kristen; Norton, Mark; Lyalin, David; Williams, Warren *et al* (authors)

p. cm.

Includes bibliographical references, glossary, appendices and index.

1. Business Rules, 2. Rule Authoring, 3. Knowledge Work, 4. Definitions of Business Terms, 5. Coordination rules, 6. Business Process Management, 7. Qualification/disqualification Rules, 8. Decision rules, 9. Business Process Innovation, 10. Internet of Things

Table of Contents

Appendices

Foreword

Business rules cover a very broad space. Across the entire space, however, you can be sure about one central idea – business logic should not be buried in procedural programming languages. Call it *rule independence*.

Why is rule independence important to you? Because rules entangled in procedural code won't ever be agile. Rules change all the time – and in a digital world the pace of change is always accelerating. How you can stay on top of it is the central question in business agility.

That's not to say that business logic is simple. Just the opposite. It can often be quite complex. So why entangle it in procedures and code, which must attend to all sorts of other complex concerns, ranging from platforming, messaging, synchronization, data access, user interfaces, and more? Why mix them up?

So, business rules are all about *disentanglement* – a natural separation of concerns. What advantages does that have? For one thing, you can involve subject matter experts directly in the validation and verification of the business logic before it is implemented. For another, you can often empower the business side to make changes directly to the business logic after deployment. In other words, you can give a degree of control back to the business side – and in the process, free up IT resources for other work.

Let's not forget about compliance. Often, they are among the strongest supporters of the business rule approach. Why? Because with business rules, results can be directly traceable. If someone (such as a business partner or regulator) wants to know *why* a business result was produced, instead of program code or (usually sparse) documentation, you can inspect the actual business rules that produced the results. Fast, efficient, trustworthy.

To understand all the areas that business rules cover requires looking at the things that business processes must (or should) address.

- *Decisions.* Suppose you want dynamic pricing, taking into account multiple factors about the customer, the product, current demand and supply, size of the order, etc. What better way to organize the business logic than as a set of rules?! You can analyze the structure of the decision using an appropriate decision model, then express the rules in some decision table(s) with clear outcomes. Recognizing that decisions are a separable part of process models has been one of the most important contributions of the business rule approach.

- *Case Management.* Businesses often organize activities around concepts that have predictable stages or states. A classic example is the medical case of a patient. The same thinking, however, pops up in a great many situations – for example, products developed in stages, orders that progress through predictable states, complaints, inquiries, break-downs, purchases, etc. What better way to coordinate allowable movement between states or stages than by explicit rules expressing what constraints must be satisfied?! Managing cases effectively as a distinct aspect of processes would prove difficult or impossible without rules.

- *Data quality.* If you want high data quality, it must reflect business results produced correctly in the first place. Business rules help ensure that happens by guiding business behavior. Think about it this way: Processes only ensure you do the correct things; business rules ensure you do those things *correctly*. So, business rules always play either a direct or an indirect role in data quality matters – there's no way to escape it. Business rules give the prominent profile to data quality matters absent in processes alone.

- *Digitalization.* Even in today's world, many gaps remain in processes where manual intervention is still required, sometimes as basic as simply moving data from one form or format to another. It the past few years, robotic process automation (RPA) has stepped up to this challenge by offering effective rule-based solutions.

Not everything business rules address, however, are so easily cast into a pure-process perspective. Nor should they be. Consider these areas:

- *Requirements.* Analysts and developers face several key challenges. One is ensuring that models are robust and complete. Put simply, diagrams are just diagrams without rules. Another is user stories. It's been said that user stories represent merely the tip of the iceberg with respect to requirements. What's the other 90%? A significant percentage is *business rules.*

- *Communication.* In a day and age when IT is so central to running business, it's simply unacceptable that communication gaps still exist between the business side and IT. How can these gaps be closed in a manner that does full service to the complexity and richness of what business people know in their heads? And to the vocabulary they use to talk about it? *Business rules.*

- *Knowledge Retention.* In traditional companies, retirement of key subject matter experts is a hard reality. In newer companies, the turn-over rate of workers is unprecedented. How do you capture core knowledge in such form that it is not lost when workers walk out the door? *Business rules.*

In thinking about all these areas that business rules address, it's hard to escape the insight that business rules are a pure form of explicit knowledge. They shape business behavior and guide decisions – independently of (but in cooperation with) procedures and platforms. What else could they be but pure business knowledge?

In a day and age when machine learning (ML) and AI are all the rage, it's fair to ask why business rules still matter. Will ML and AI make business rules obsolete? If not, where is the dividing line between them?

There's no doubt that we're just at the beginning of a wild and exciting ride for how machines will address knowledge. In certain respects, however, the shape of things to come is already clear. And the answer is *no*, ML and AI will *not* make business rules obsolete. Let me explain why.

Today's ML capabilities are purely statistical. In fact, that's the very reason for the unbelievable progress AI has made over the last decade – the realization that many problems do *not* actually require symbolic representation (think *words*). A bot driving a car does not need to explain why it didn't hit a pedestrian – it just needs not to hit them. A bot listening to my voice commands does not need to explain why it 'knows' it's talking to me – it just needs to be sure it's me. A bot playing a game of chess or Go does not need to explain its moves – it just needs to win.

And that brings us to the bottom line for business rules – they always tell you *why*. Whenever humans are in the loop – and there are explicit laws and obligations and rules to worry about – you'll always need to know *why*. That's what business rules are ultimately about – the *why*.

I could go on, but enough about the ideas behind business rules and their role in the industry. I'm pretty sure you're reading this book to find out what world-class practitioners have actually achieved in their businesses with business rules. So, let's get to it!

You're going to be hugely impressed by the range of industries and problem spaces addressed by the case studies in this book. I know I am. I've gotten all sorts of new ideas from them – and I'm sure you will too. Enjoy!

Ronald G. Ross
Co-Founder & Principal, Business Rule Solutions, LLC
Executive Editor, BRCommunity.com

Introduction and Overview

Layna Fischer, Future Strategies Inc.

WHAT ARE BUSINESS RULES?

Definition: A business rule defines or constrains some aspect of business and always resolves to either true or false. It specifically involves terms, facts and rules. Business rules are intended to assert business structure or to control or influence the behavior of the business.

Business rules describe the operations, definitions and constraints that apply to an organization. Business rules can apply to people, processes, corporate behavior and computing systems in an organization, and are put in place to help the organization achieve its goals. Even though a system of strategic processes govern business rules, business rules are not strategic themselves; they are directive.[1]

WHY SHOULD WE USE THEM?

This book helps corporate business readers to understand the meaning and impact of Business Rules within a variety of applications or scenarios such as:

- Why and how to use a rules-based approach to validate, transform, recalculate, and remediate complex applications
- The art of managing rules and terminology in a consistent, business-friendly, and shareable way
- How to use rules engine to achieve uniformity, consistency, continuous monitoring, transparency, flexibility, forecasting etc.
- Some of the key technologies, vendors and implementers in this ecosystem.

FOREWORD

Ronald Ross, Co-Founder & Principal, Business Rule Solutions, LLC

Business rules cover a very broad space. Across the entire space, however, you can be sure about one central idea – business logic should not be buried in procedural programming languages. Call it *rule independence.*

Why is rule independence important to you? Because rules entangled in procedural code won't ever be agile. Rules change all the time – and in a digital world the pace of change is always accelerating. How you can stay on top of it is the central question in business agility.

To understand all the areas that business rules cover requires looking at the things that business processes must (or should) address.

---

[1] https://en.wikipedia.org/wiki/Business_rule

Part 1: Rules and Relationships

FOCUS ON WHAT MAKES YOUR BUSINESS SMART

Gladys S.W. Lam, Principal and Co-Founder of Business Rules Solutions, USA

This opening chapter tackles the five components that make your business smart:
- operational strategies
- business concepts
- business rules
- operational business decisions
- key performance indicators

Collectively, these elements are referred to as the Operational IP (Intellectual Property) of your business. An organizations is always in various stages of managing its Operational IP. The author discusses one of the most talked-about components in your Operational IP: business rules.

COLLABORATIVE RULE AUTHORING

Kristen Seer, Senior Business Rules Analyst, Business Rules Solutions, USA

Large-scale rule harvesting projects present many challenges, from partitioning the work among a cadre of business analysts (BAs), to coordinating the work overtime, to delivering high-quality business rules. The keys to success lie in proper planning, strict adherence to a well-defined business vocabulary, following best practices in rule authoring, and constant communication amongst the Bas. This chapter describes the challenges of harvesting many rules from disparate sources and how they were overcome by the project team to produce a successful outcome that delighted the clients.

THE CASE OF THE MISSING ALGORITHM

Mark Norton, CEO & Founder, IDIOM Limited, New Zealand

There are a small number of core concepts that can be said to embody the essence of an enterprise. This chapter asserts that one such concept is the business algorithm, the unique combination of business logic, algebra, and rules that is used by the enterprise to convert real world data and events into useful outcomes that benefit all stakeholders – giving rise to contented customers, prosperous proprietors, and satisfied staff!

The business algorithm is a unique and fundamentally important concept that no enterprise can function without. There are other aspects of the enterprise like brand or culture that may also claim to be 'of the essence', but the business algorithm is the only such concept that has a formal existence inside computer systems. The business algorithm is like the soul of the enterprise, uniquely defining the enterprise and giving it life via its systems.

EVALUATION OF PATIENT ELIGIBILITY FOR PUBLICLY-FUNDED VACCINES

David Lyalin, Public Health Analyst, Centers for Disease Control and Prevention (CDC), USA
Warren Williams, Branch Chief (retired), Centers for Disease Control and Prevention (CDC), USA

Federal, state, and local government immunization programs in the United States provide publicly-funded vaccines to eligible patients, with the largest of these programs being the federally-funded Vaccines for Children (VFC) program. In this month's feature, Dr. David Lyalin and Warren Williams of the CDC (Centers for Disease Control and Prevention) present a case study that applies business rules and decision tables techniques to document recommendations for evaluating a patient's eligibility for publicly-funded immunization programs and private coverage.

Part 2: Business Rules in Action
Award-Winning Case Studies

A CALIFORNIA BANK, USA

Nominated by OpenRules, Inc., USA

This case study describes a successful implementation of business rules within a large California bank[2] with 80 billion in assets. The bank needed to modernize the existing onboarding system by adding over 600 new, dynamically-formulated KYC (Know Your Customer) questions. The new interaction logic was very complex, requiring the complicated UI to be dynamically modified for different types of customers, accounts, and planned account activities. The questions to be asked were dependent on previously-provided answers and already-known information about customers and their accounts. Hard-coding of such interaction logic into the existing onboarding system would be both cost- and time-prohibitive. Instead, a radically new approach driven by externalized rules was implemented to significantly reduce implementation and maintenance costs as well as delivery timelines.

In the face of encountered difficulties with no solutions available on the one hand, and looming regulatory fines, on the other hand, the bank had to drastically rethink and seek for a solution that could still work. They opted for a solution that could utilize an off-the-shelf rules-based framework to meet complexity of the requirements. As a result, the new system was developed, tested, and deployed on the bank's production servers using rules-based web application and web services frameworks.

DELOITTE LIMITED (NEW ZEALAND)

Nominated by IDIOM Limited, New Zealand

Deloitte Limited (New Zealand) provides professional services including payroll remediation services to clients throughout New Zealand. NZ enacted complex holiday and termination payment rules in the Holidays Act 2003 that payroll systems have generally failed to implement correctly. The law requires remediation for the last six-years of payroll.

Deloitte has so far remediated the payrolls for more than 20 employers across the country (both public and private), hundreds of thousands of employees, and eight underlying payroll platforms.

This submission describes how Deloitte's use of rules has given it an agile and cost-effective process to recalculate and remediate payroll systems at scale. The NZ Police case is used as a reference case to highlight key elements of the solution described herein.

---

[2] The financial institution requested anonymity

DUTCH ROAD AUTHORITIES, TRAFFIC CONTROL, THE NETHERLANDS

Nominated by LibRT, The Netherlands

Rule-based traffic management is a methodology for dynamic traffic management that is a joint development of the different road authorities (municipal, state, central government) in the Netherlands and the major suppliers of the road authorities.

A better way is using declarative business rules that describe what must, may and can be done to improve a traffic situation. Typically, we promote the outbound flow, decrease inbound flow or reroute traffic. The new approach is simple, easy to maintain and connected to the policies agreed between the road authorities in a region.

A prerequisite of automated execution is the availability of actual and reliable traffic data. A national data center collects and distributes traffic data of different sources. Road authorities use this data to execute the automated rules.

IBM GLOBAL SALES INCENTIVES

Nominated by IBM Corporation, USA

Like many corporations, IBM is moving to Robotics Processing Automation (RPA) to accomplish repeatable mundane administrative tasks. The Global Sales Incentives (GSI) organization within IBM has embraced RPA as a means to move work off of sales managers and sales incentives support personnel, freeing them up to perform higher value type activities.

Using Robotics Processing Automation (RPA) software, the IBM Global Sales Incentives (GSI) team created an automated process to have a robot work as a delegate to sales managers to create 2H 2017 Incentive Plan Letters (IPL) for sellers on a specific type of plan known as a Pool Plan. The IPL is the formal agreement between IBM and each person who is eligible to be on an incentive plan.

Having a robot to follow a specific set of business rules and creating the IPLs for 2H 2017 Pool Plans freed those sales managers up from manually entering data from other systems into the system where the IPLs are created and tracked, allowing them more time for other more productive engagements with their sellers and clients.

IISSB AT CDC, USA

Nominated by CDC/IISSB, Immunization Information Systems Support Branch, USA

The Immunization Information Systems Support Branch (IISSB) at the Centers for Disease Control and Prevention (CDC) "works to maximize protection against vaccine-preventable diseases by leading the advancement of immunization information systems (IIS). Immunization information systems help to maximize protection against vaccine-preventable diseases by providing accurate data on which to make informed immunization decisions".[i]

The IISSB provides guidance and information to the IIS community in the form of IIS functional standards, guidelines, specifications, and recommendations.

KPN, THE NETHERLANDS

Nominated by Aura Portal, Spain

KPN is the largest Dutch telecom and network provider with over 7.8 million mobile subscribers in the Netherlands and provides broadband access to 4.1 million customers offering business services and data transport network throughout Western Europe. KPN offers their customers the most extensive IP network in the Netherlands providing optimal coverage.

KPN Network Provider is facing a strong growth of business and network-capacity services and an accompanying increase of operational costs. KPN Network Provider transformed their existing and complex fulfilment IT to support the rapidly changing market.

Overall, the achieved results are remarkable, positively impacting fulfilment efficiency for Core Roll-Out Delivery (reduced workload and achieved process control and monitoring) and other areas.

MMG INSURANCE, USA

Nominated by EA Department, MMG Insurance, USA

Three years ago, MMG Insurance began a business transformation journey involving legacy system replacement and a customer-facing portal modernization. MMG's future growth plan required that the technology platform supporting MMG's core business processes be robust, agile, and scalable. In partnership with their core system vendor and several third parties, they completed the first part of this journey in February 2018; with the replacement of our billing system.

Challenges came with their core system vendor having teams offshore in India and others in the US. Conflicting terminology was used among internal and vendor teams, and management of rules varied. Miscommunication occurred, whether face-to-face, during conference calls, or in hand-offs of documentation.

To combat this, they leaned on their dedication to managing rules and terminology in a consistent, business-friendly, and shareable way, by using a business rule management tool to create a single source of truth. Effective business rule and terminology management was instrumental in MMG being fully operational on day one.

POWERHEALTH SOLUTIONS,

Nominated by IDIOM Limited, New Zealand

PowerHealth Solutions (Australia) [PHS] provides its "PowerPerformance Manager" and "PowerBilling and Revenue Collection" [PBRC] applications to healthcare organizations worldwide as 'Commercial Off the Shelf' [COTS] applications.

PHS started a rules initiative in 2004 that is the subject of this submission, with the objective of making costing/revenue and billing rules a plug-n-play feature within their applications. The separation of rules from the underlying applications was required to allow PHS to support bespoke customer rules within their otherwise standard applications.

This submission uses the development of PBRC for the HKHA as a reference project for the initiative, to highlight the benefits of using rules as a formal architectural component within COTS applications.

RABOBANK, THE NETHERLANDS

Nominated by Oracle, The Netherlands

Rabobank is an international financial services provider operating on the basis of cooperative principles. As a cooperative bank, Rabobank is a socially-responsible bank. It serves approximately 8.7 million clients around the world and is one of the largest cooperatives in the Netherlands with nearly two million members. Members are more than just customers; they have a voice in deciding the bank's strategic course. Rabobank is committed to making a substantial contribution towards achieving wealth and prosperity in the Netherlands and to resolving the food issue worldwide.

Having a business rules solution enabled Rabobank to get a major concern, Customer Due Diligence, under control, in a relative short period of time. The benefits are huge and versatile: real-time & batch wise checking, performing over millions of records, traceability of decisions, auditability, consistency in logic, flexibility in business logic changes and last, but not least, predictability of impact of rule changes.

UNITED SERVICES AUTOMOBILE ASSOCIATION (USAA), USA

Nominated by USAA, United States

It is imperative for a company to know what the business is doing. To accomplish this, business professionals must take responsibility for knowing what the business does. The project quite simply was to build a business rules repository.

Several years ago, USAA, Property & Casualty Company, embarked on a journey to engineer and document their business rules to capture intellectual capital and preserve corporate memory. The building of a business rules repository is an investment that takes time and people, and in the end, its value is priceless. Their users of a business rules repository are vast - underwriters, product managers, defect managers, development and execution owners, experience owners, insurance compliance owners, competitive intelligence owners and quality assurance analysts.

In addition to engineering business rules, the team has begun exploring system architecture to provide further benefit to their users. Including business rules in a system architecture model at points where they impact processes broadens the user's understanding of the business as a whole. The impetus for beginning their business rules journey was the replacement of a legacy IT system.

Section 1

Business Rules
Management

Focusing on What Makes Your Business Smart: *Business Rules*

Gladys S. W. Lam, Business Rule Solutions, LLC

Think about what makes you smart. You are smart when you make the right decisions or behave intelligently.

You might not realize it, but you learn to behave intelligently through the rules you were given since you were young. When you were six months old and were just about to pick up that piece of junk on the floor to put in your mouth, your mother said, "NO! Don't do that!". That was a behavioral rule your mother gave you to prevent you from getting sick. Obeying that rule was a smart thing to do. Next time you saw a piece of interesting article on the floor, you had to make a decision. Do I put it in my mouth? What would be the right decision? There was a rule to guide you. Do the smart thing. Listen to the rule.

Now think about your business environment. What makes your business smart?

When your business builds or revises a business capability, what do your business stakeholders concentrate on? Natural areas are:

- People – We need good people. Human Resource Departments have been around for a long time. They are set up to help manage people.
- Technologies – Technologies have been around since before the invention of machines. Organizations are familiar with dealing with technology changes.
- Information – That was a big deal in the 1980s and 1990s during the height of the information management era. Today, big data is the hot topic in many organizations.
- Process – Business process management and business process re-engineering have been popular since the 1990s. There are many techniques offered in this area.

Are these things really enough to make your business smart? Not entirely. Something very important is missing.

- A process may be efficient, but it is the guidance to avoid mistakes and to make intelligent judgements that makes a capability smart.
- Information may be collected and managed, but it is how the information is used to make proper decisions that makes a capability smart.
- Technology may be state-of-the-art, but it is the application of the technologies to guide behaviour and operations that makes a capability smart.
- People may be working at maximum capacity, but it is their knowledge that makes a capability smart.

What is the fifth piece that completes the pie and makes your business capability smart?

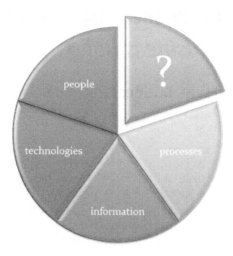

From the 'junk on the floor' story, you might guess it's rules and decisions. A business capability is smart when it enables people, technologies, information, and processes to behave intelligently and safely, and to make the right decisions.

Altogether, there are actually five components needed to make your business capability smart and produce maximum benefit:

- business rules
- operational business decisions
- operational strategies
- business concepts
- key performance indicators

Collectively, we refer to these five areas as your business knowledge.

Organizations are in the various stages of managing their business knowledge. In this discussion, I will explore one of the most frequently neglected components in your knowledge: business rules.

WHAT'S A BUSINESS RULE?

One of the best parts of my job is the opportunity to visit major organizations worldwide. In guiding organizations in adopting a business rules approach, one of the first things that becomes very apparent is that different people have different perceptions of business rules. So, if you are embarking on a project focusing on business rules, do not assume everyone knows what a business rule is or assume everyone thinks about business rules the same way you do.

- Some people might think business rules are requirements: e.g., "Provide a feature to handle electronic funds transfer."

- Some people might think business rules are use case statements: e.g., "Customer provides account ID. System displays account information."

- Some people might think business rules are system 'if/then' statements: e.g., "If the overdrawn flag is set to 'yes', then reject transaction."

So, what is a business rule? The definition I like is:

A business rule is a criterion used in business operations to:

- *guide behavior*

- *make decisions*[1]

By that definition, the business rules related to the above requirement, use case, and system 'if/then' statement respectively might be:
- "Each employee expense reimbursement must be processed through electronic funds transfer."
- "A customer must have a valid account ID."
- "An account must not be overdrawn." "An account may be considered overdrawn only if the amount of a cash withdrawal is greater than the balance of the account at the time of the withdrawal."

Notice how the business rule statements above are about the business, not the system. A business rules approach makes you ask the business questions first. Your business needs these business rules even if there are no automated systems.

Remember that business rules guide your business operation. A business rule tells you what you may or may not do in daily business activity.

WHAT'S THE BIG DEAL?

Haven't we been implementing business rules since the beginning of time?

Yes, of course! We have always implemented rules. You need the right payroll calculation rules to calculate the correct payroll amounts. You need the right distribution rules to ensure the correct inventory is sent out of the right warehouse.

So, what is the big deal? The big deal is that with the advent of technology and the digital age, there is a need to make change faster – especially the need to change business rules quickly in order to keep up with business needs. The problems with traditional approaches are:
- Business rules are imbedded in systems.
- Business people don't know their business rules.
- Business people have no control over their business rules.
- Business people cannot manage their business rules.

If your business needs to change a business rule, it can no longer afford to wait 6 months, 3 months, or even 1 week for IT to make a change. In order to stay competitive and to provide customer service in this rapid-paced age, it is imperative that the business side has the ability to:
- Know what the business rules are.
- Assess the impact of changing those rules.
- Make appropriate changes to the rules quickly.

Given the continuous evolution of business needs and the IT industry, business rule management is crucial. Ask yourself this: Once a business has power over its data, what would it want next?

Data is passive. It is after the fact. You can build enormous data warehouses to analyze your data. You will know your customer trends, your product sales and your employee behaviors. But what good is knowing all that if you can't act on it? What's the solution? Business rules!

Remember business rules tell your business what you may or may not do. You change and enforce behavior and decisions through business rules. Business rules help make your business smart!

For example

You discover from your data that the slowest period in your retail store is 8:00am to 9:00am. You figure you have two options to increase profitability:

1. To generate business during those hours, you could introduce an early-bird morning sale – 20% off all items in the store between 8:00am to 9:00am.
2. To save costs, change the opening hours to 9:00am.

Your business simply cannot afford to wait a long time for these changes. You want to be able to introduce discounts or reschedule workers in real time. What if this store is only part of a chain of stores? How quickly can you act? How quickly can you analyze the impact of this change?

A business rules approach gives the business the capability to identify, analyze, implement, and manage change like this in a timely and efficient manner.

WHERE'S THE CHALLENGE?

Business rules are rules about the business. So, it doesn't take a rocket scientist to tell you that business rules should come from the business (i.e., that business people, not IT, should specify the business rules).

Traditionally, IT gathers rules from the business. It then goes away and hides for months on end and finally, converts those rules into a language that takes a university degree to understand. The business is too intimidated to challenge those rules – or the techies that created them. IT is viewed as mystical. Any rule change requires a formal invitation to the wizards to come out and do their magic. (Then you pray it will actually work.)

This doesn't fly anymore in today's environment. Desktop and mobile computing enable business people to be their own wizards. You should see some of the Excel spreadsheets I have reviewed! Business people want more control. A business rules approach enables that.

Now, back to what is actually hard about business rules. The business rules are hard *to find* – that's what. Every business we go to has business rules – hundreds and thousands of rules. So, where are they? In people's heads, in existing code written by the technical wizards of yesteryear, in policy manuals, in outdated user guides, etc. So, what's hard is specifying the right business rules for the right things.

WHAT'S THE SOLUTION?

A simplistic answer is to buy better packaged software. I have seen too many organizations fall into the trap of buying software in the hopes of solving their problems. Millions of dollars are spent on technology skills to learn how to use it. What's always forgotten is how the business side fits in.

In order to build a smart business capability, you need a solid approach to gather, analyze and manage business rules. The key to success lies with the thinking about what to put in a tool, not simply the tool itself. Giving MS Word to someone does not magically enable the person to write. The tool gives you bells and whistles, but without the right content, it's still useless.

Embarking on a business rules approach is no different. Simply acquiring a powerful rules or decision engine does not guarantee success. There are many excellent business rule and decision management tools in the market today. Don't get me wrong. The tool is important. The technology exists. The real benefit to a business rules approach, however, is its ability to connect the business directly to its business rules.

The key is knowing how to gather and manage business rules from the business and how to connect them to technology implementations.

This is where I believe business analysts can make a significant difference. Business analysts play a major role in:

1. Capturing business rules from:
   - Subject area experts, in facilitated sessions or one-on-one interviews
   - Documentation, by identifying processes, decisions and policies and by asking the right questions to extract business rules
   - System code, by reversing engineering system logic to business logic and by distinguishing business rules from system rules

2. Specifying business rules by:
   - Writing business rule statements in a consistent manner
   - Developing business-based decision structures
   - Creating business-friendly decision tables

3. Analyzing business rules for:
   - Duplication, redundancy, subsumption, and conflicts
   - Impact to existing rules when a rule is changed, deleted or added
   - Reuse of existing business rules instead of creating new ones for each initiative or each business area

4. Managing business rules to:
   - Provide governance when business rule changes are needed
   - Organize a large set of business rules
   - Report on business rules from different perspectives
   - Establish relationship between business rules or business rule sets
   - Set up traceability of business rules from source to implementation

WHAT'S NEXT?

In this discussion I concentrated mostly on business rules. Business rules are often the entry point to the other areas in your business knowledge. One of those is operational business decisions. I encourage you to take advantage of our free white papers on that topic. You can also find out more about organizing and engineering business knowledge from our blogs, articles, books, training, and conferences.

SUMMARY

Remember …
- Your business knowledge makes your business smart.
- Business rules are a central component of your business knowledge.

- Your business rules return power to the business to drive business solutions.

Business knowledge completes the pie graph presented earlier. Focus on what makes your business smart. It takes all five elements build a smart business capability.

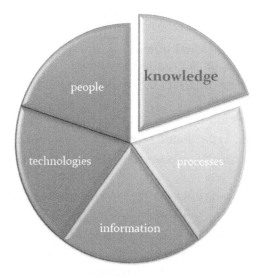

---

[1] ***Building Business Solutions: Business Analysis with Business Rules***, by Ronald G. Ross with Gladys S.W. Lam, An **IIBA® Sponsored Handbook**, Business Rule Solutions, LLC, October 2011, 244 pp.

URL: http://www.brsolutions.com/bbs

Collaborative Rule Authoring

Kristen Seer, Business Rule Solutions, LLC, USA

INTRODUCTION

Large-scale rule harvesting projects present a unique set of challenges, from partitioning the work amongst a cadre of business analysts (BAs) to delivering high-quality, well-organized business rules. The keys to success lie in proper planning, strict adherence to a well-defined business vocabulary, use of best practices in rule authoring, and constant communication amongst the BAs.

On a re-platforming project for a large financial organization, the task was to harvest complex business rules for determining eligibility for mortgages[1]. The rules were scattered across multiple sources such as business requirement documents, use cases, application code, data dictionaries, etc. To add to the complexity, the rules needed to be harvested from two separate applications that were being re-platformed and that contained what were essentially duplicate business rules.

Because the organization did not have a structured approach for such a rule-intensive initiative, they brought in our consulting firm as we had a well-established business rules methodology and a team of experienced business rule analysts (of which I was one).

One the of key business problems the client wanted to address was the discrepancy in the business rules implemented in the two application systems. Although the systems contained what were essentially the same rules, their outcomes were often significantly different. As these were customer-facing applications, this resulted in increasing levels of customer dissatisfaction. The strategy to solve this problem was to externalize the business rules, store them in a central repository, and then ensure any changes were reflected in both systems as appropriate.

This case study describes the challenges of harvesting a large number of rules from disparate sources and how they were overcome by the project team to produce a successful outcome that delighted the clients. It outlines the project approach and activities for the following phases:

- Preparation
- High-Level Business Analysis
- Daily Routine
- Weekly Status
- Validation.

The last section summarizes the lessons learned from our experience.

PREPARATION

A significant factor in the success of the project was the emphasis placed on up-front preparation. This included:

- Assembling the team
- Defining scope
- Identifying sources
- Determining what to capture

---

[1] The examples used in the chapter are similar to, but not exactly the same as, deliverables produced on the project.

- Organizing the rules
- Partitioning the work

Assembling the Team

A project manager with extensive experience in managing rule harvesting projects initiated the project and assembled the team.

A virtual team of five BAs (of which I was one) — all with years of experience in rule authoring — was put together from Canada, U.S., Europe and Asia.

A small team of subject matter experts (SMEs) was assigned by the client on a part-time basis to be available to answer questions and resolve issues throughout the rule-harvesting process.

A larger team of SMEs were brought on board during the validation phase to divide the work of reviewing hundreds of business rules into smaller, more manageable tasks.

Defining Scope

With business rule projects, a small change in scope can result in a significant increase in the number of business rules that need to be harvested. Although the scope went through several iterations, most of these were during the up-front planning process. Our project manager ensured the scope was very well defined and that all the BAs were vigilant in keeping within scope during the entire project.

Identifying Sources

With two separate application systems being re-platformed, there were several potential sources available for the rules. However, most of them were project artifacts (use cases, requirements, etc.) that had not been kept up to date. A further complication was that the two systems had been developed by external software companies that were reluctant to divulge what they considered to be their intellectual property (even though the rules themselves truly belonged to the client!).

The most accurate and up-to-date sources for the rules were identified and these became the "trusted" sources. This was a time-consuming task as it proved difficult to get the most recent versions of the documents. Other documents were used as secondary sources in case of conflicts or inconsistencies in the trusted sources. As a last resort, the software companies were consulted to determine what had actually been implemented. Over time, the vendors began to understand what we needed and were able to supply us with the appropriate pieces of application code (such as error messages, which turned out to be the most useful way to reengineer some of the rules).

Determining What to Capture

In any rules project, there should be consideration given to any additional information that needs to be captured for each business rule. This includes considering *why* the information is needed and whether the reason justifies the cost of maintaining the information over time. In this case, we decided to capture:

- clear traceability from source to implementation,
- statuses to track the lifecycle of the rules, and
- guidance for when a rule was breached, whether a message or an action needed to be taken.

Thinking about this up-front ensured that we didn't need to backtrack partway through the project to capture information that was essential. It also helped to set expectations with the client as to the deliverables.

Organizing the Rules

When faced with harvesting hundreds of rules, it's important to choose some basis on which to organize the rules so they are not overwhelming, both for the BAs and the SMEs. Because the rules were about determining eligibility, we decided to group the rules based on the decision structure. (See Figure 1 for a partial decision structure.) This really helped break down the complexity and enabled the BA's to focus on small sets of rules at a time.

Partitioning the Work

Because there were so many BAs on the team, it was important to partition the work so that there was minimal overlap in the rules. The decision structure proved to be an ideal way to partition the rules as there was very little overlap between each sub-decision.

In addition, one BA was designated to manage the concept model in a role we affectionately called "The Terminator" because she had to be tough on compliance with the terminology. She was responsible for updating both the concept model diagrams (see Figure 2 for an example) and the definitions as well as ensuring all the BAs were using the proper terminology in the business rules.

HIGH-LEVEL BUSINESS ANALYSIS

High-level business analysis was done with the client including facilitated sessions to determine the decision structure. This phase consisted of:

- Analyzing the decisions
- Building the vocabulary
- Identifying rule patterns
- Writing "overarching" rules

Analyzing the Decisions

The core decision of determining eligibility was analyzed using a technique called Q-Charts. This enabled the main decision to be broken down into smaller, more manageable sub-decisions. The decision structure was validated with the SMEs. Although there were some changes to the structure over the course of the project, it remained quite stable and served as a means to help keep within scope, partition the work, and organize the business rules.

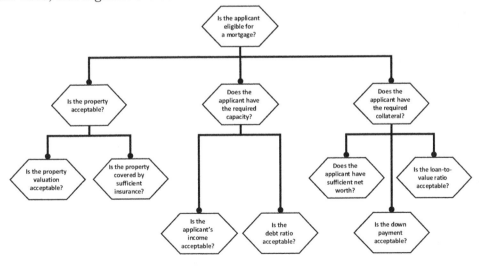

Figure 1: Sample Decision Structure

Building the Vocabulary

From the very beginning of the project, the BAs started capturing the business vocabulary and building a concept model. (See Figure 2 for a simplified concept model containing some relevant terms.) At this point, only the key terms were modeled. The SMEs were enlisted to provide existing definitions wherever possible and to validate the concept model and definitions.

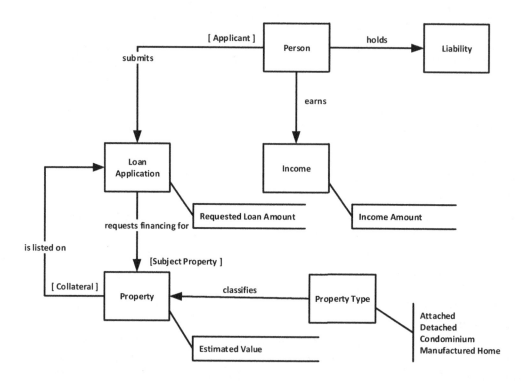

Figure 2: Sample Concept Model

Identifying Rule Patterns

In order to have a similar "look and feel" for the rules (so that the reviewers weren't faced with a different writing style from each BA), we used RuleSpeak™ which provided us with basic guidelines and templates to structure the rules.

In addition, we were able to identify some patterns or commonalities amongst the rules. For example, determining the value of a property may differ based on the property type (detached, condominium, etc.), but the overall structure of the rules is very similar. This enabled us to have more detailed templates available which both sped up the writing process and greatly contributed to the consistency of the rules.

We were also able to identify opportunities to use decision tables, particularly as there were several already implemented across the two application systems. As these were quite complex, we did some analysis on how they might be simplified to be more comprehensible.

Writing Overarching Rules

The last step was to capture what we sometimes refer to as "overarching" rules. These cover two kinds of rules that were shared across the decision. The first kind involved basic calculations and derivations that were reused in several places throughout the decision structure. We also identified "showstoppers" (i.e., rules that preempted the need to determine eligibility such as the borrower being under a certain age, or a property type (e.g., manufactured home) excluded from the kind of mortgage within scope of the eligibility decision.

DAILY ROUTINE

At least once a week (but often more frequently), all the BA's and sometimes the PM would hold a conference call. This was challenging due to time zones, as for some it was first thing in the morning, while for others it was the end of their day.

The main topic was vocabulary, followed by specific issues with the rules. Our Terminator made sure we were all kept up to date with any changes to the concept model, and we discussed any new terms that had come up during our rule authoring so they could be incorporated into the concept model. This was a significant task as, over time, the concept model grew to more than 1,000 terms!

Any issues that needed the input of the SMEs were logged. Some of these were resolved via email, but the more complex ones were saved for discussion at the weekly status meeting.

These team calls proved to be invaluable, enabling the BAs to work as a well-formed team and really support each other.

The rest of the day was spent writing rules. Some days one might write only a handful of rules while working out some complex decision logic, while other days might produce several dozen, especially if the rules followed one of the pre-defined patterns. On difficult days, one could go down the wrong path and have to throw the work away. These occasions were rare and often averted because of the ability to share our thinking in the team calls.

We always focused first on the core rules and then dealt with exceptions. As one of my favorite authors, Fritz Leiber, once said, "Exceptions to general rules are only doorways to further knowledge and finer classifications."

WEEKLY STATUS

Each week, some of the team (it varied based on the agenda) met virtually with the client to provide an update on status and bring forth any unresolved issues. Issues were documented, tracked and followed-up to ensure they were resolved in a timely manner.

VALIDATION

As each set of rules was completed for a sub-decision, an internal review was conducted to ensure:

- The rules used the defined terminology
- The rules followed the pre-defined patterns and/or RuleSpeak™
- There were no anomalies in the rules (i.e., no duplicates, overlaps, conflicts, etc.)

Once all the rules were harvested, they needed to be validated by the SMEs. This was a highly organized effort with the large team of SMEs being split up into smaller groups based on their expertise. Each team was assigned a set of rules with the accompanying vocabulary to review. The PM and some of the BAs were onsite to coordinate the logistics, answer any questions, and incorporate any changes requested by the SMEs.

In many ways, validation was the most gratifying phase as this was where all the BAs' discipline and hard work paid off. Many of the SMEs were surprised that it was a whole team that had written the rules, commenting that the rules were so consistent they were sure that one person had written them all! With the well-defined terminology and rule patterns/templates, they found the rules easy to validate as any issues (incompleteness, inaccuracies, duplications, etc.) seemed to stand out.

CONCLUSION

This project employed proven business rule methodologies and techniques that provided a solid framework and enabled the team to produce high-quality, well-organized business rules.

But as sound as the approach was, the success of the project really came down to three factors:

- A Project Manager highly experienced in rule harvesting projects
- Business Analysts extremely disciplined in using the terminology and rule patterns in authoring the rules
- Subject Matter Experts willing to devote the time to review hundreds of rules.

Challenges were overcome through open communication, a willingness to explore unknown territory, and a collaborative approach focused on solving problems.

As a Business Analyst, I've had the opportunity to work on many projects across numerous industries, but I still count my experience on this one as a highlight of my career.

REFERENCES

The following are good sources for the methodologies and techniques referenced in this chapter:

RuleSpeak™: www.rulespeak.com

Concept Model: *Business Knowledge Blueprints: Enabling Your Data to Speak the Language of the Business* by Ronald G. Ross, 2019

Q-Charts: *Decision Analysis: A Primer – How to Use DecisionSpeak™ and Question Charts (Q-Charts™)* by Ronald G. Ross, 2013.

The Case of the Missing Algorithm

Mark Norton, Idiom Software, New Zealand

AND WHAT HAS HAECCEITY GOT TO DO WITH IT?

Meet Quiddity and Haecceity

'Quiddity' and 'Haecceity' are two unusual words that aren't often used in daily conversation – especially IT conversations.

Which is a pity because they exactly describe a concept that is an important factor in successful delivery of commercial IT systems.

Let's see what the words actually mean[1]:

Quiddity[2]: "The real nature of a thing; the essence"

Haecceity[3]: "The property that uniquely identifies an object."

While the definitions are closely aligned, the slight difference is material to this conversation.

This time from Wikipedia[4]:

> "Haecceity may be defined in some dictionaries as simply the 'essence' of a thing, or as a simple synonym for quiddity. However, such a definition deprives the term of its subtle distinctiveness and utility. Whereas *haecceity* refers to aspects of a thing that make it a particular thing, *quiddity* refers to the universal qualities of a thing, its 'whatness', or the aspects of a thing it may share with other things and by which it may form part of a genus of things."

To provide relevance to this conversation, we need to clarify what thing or object we are talking about – and that thing or object is the enterprise itself, in whole or in part.

There are a small number of core concepts that can be said to embody the essence of an enterprise. This article asserts that one such concept is the business algorithm, the unique combination of business logic, algebra, and rules that is used by the enterprise to convert real world data and events into useful outcomes that benefit all stakeholders – giving rise to contented customers, prosperous proprietors, and satisfied staff!

In keeping with the definition of quiddity, the business algorithm will have numerous common constructs that are readily identifiable as being 'of the domain' and which are generally shared across participants in the domain, so that (for instance) insurance systems have degrees of sameness that are shared worldwide. As a specific example, the idea of 'earning premium' is universal and has the same implementation (more or less) in systems everywhere.

Then, in keeping with the uniqueness definition of haecceity, the general domain algorithm is extended by unique constructs that further and uniquely describe

---

[1] TheFreeDictionary.com

[2] https://www.thefreedictionary.com/quiddity

[3] https://www.thefreedictionary.com/Haecceity

[4] https://en.wikipedia.org/wiki/Haecceity

each specific enterprise. For instance, how risk is accepted and priced (underwriting and rating) is usually calculated according to the particular requirements of the owning enterprise – for instance, insurance product definitions.

The business algorithm is a unique and fundamentally important concept that no enterprise can function without. There are other aspects of the enterprise like brand or culture that may also claim to be 'of the essence', but the business algorithm is the only such concept that has a formal existence inside computer systems. The business algorithm is like the soul of the enterprise, uniquely defining the enterprise and giving it life via its systems. As such it has a unique claim to relevance as a first-order systems requirements artefact.

WHAT IS THE BUSINESS ALGORITHM?

The expansive description of the business algorithm asserted by this article was not part of the rules lexicon when we started our decisioning journey in 2001. The concept of a single artefact that embodies all business logic, algebra, and rules across the depth and breadth of an enterprise is too big and too all-encompassing to seem plausible.

But plausible it is! Hands-on development of business algorithms at this scale over the past decade has empirically demonstrated the practicality of the concept, and furthermore, it has delivered outstanding ROI outcomes in doing so.

Simply put, the business algorithm is all of the business logic, algebra, and rules that transform raw data into useful outcomes across the full extent of the subject enterprise – and yes, it is a *big thing*. What makes it viable today as a first order requirements artefact is use of a topology to break-down the complete business algorithm into manageable, business aligned units-of-work. Each unit-of-work should represent a distinct subset of the enterprise. There is no existing and agreed term for these units-of-work, so we will use our own term for them, viz. decision models. In aggregate, these decision models, each of which is a properly formed and separately executable sub-assembly of business logic, algebra, and rules within the overall business algorithm, describe a single, correct, consistent, and complete business algorithm that spans the enterprise.

We consider the business algorithm to be the supreme business requirement from a systems perspective because we can and should build the algorithm in its entirety without consideration of existing or future systems, and without regard to technology now or in the future. It is a purely business artefact that does not require IT input to develop and test. It defines explicitly and exactly the value proposition of the enterprise independently of any systems that might implement it.

For the sake of clarity, the business algorithm that is the subject of this article manifests as a distinct 'thing' – it is a tangible, user accessible model of business behaviour, self-documenting and empirically testable.

When we have the fully-formed business algorithm in our hands (so to speak), we can inspect it to infer the inbound data requirements (the 'real-world' data that drives the algorithm); and similarly, we can inspect it to identify the outbound data that defines the 'useful outcomes', which are the purpose of the algorithm.

Note that this data is discovered as a natural consequence of defining the algorithm. However, the inverse is not true – the algorithm is never discoverable as a consequence of defining the data. In this way, the algorithm becomes the primary source of data requirements.

And when we understand the inbound and outbound data requirements, then we can further infer processes that are required to efficiently acquire the inbound data (in response to external events), and to respond to the 'useful outcomes' as and when they are generated by the algorithm. The business algorithm is therefore also a primary source of process requirements, albeit transitively via the data.

How Does this Differ from Traditional Approaches?

This contrasts with traditional approaches, which put the data and/or processes in a superior position to the business logic, algebra, and rules that together form the business algorithm. In fact, some versions of OMG's UML appear to specifically exclude the business algorithm from consideration. Reference version 1.5 section 3:22:3 viz.:

"Additional compartments may be supplied as a tool extension to show other pre-defined or user defined model properties (for example to show business rules…) …but UML does not define them…"

The consequence of treating business logic, algebra, and rules as dependent properties of data and/or processes is that the enterprise knowledge and requirements that the business algorithm represents are scattered across systems, processes, and data in such a way that it is often infeasible, if not impossible, to accurately re-collate them.

They are more or less lost to view, hence the title of this article.

Our own experience in harvesting the business algorithm from existing systems shows that the scattered logic is often hard to find and re-collate, and even when found is likely to include inconsistencies, missing edge cases, redundant implementations of the same thing, and/or outright conflict, wherein multiple implementations give different answers for the same underlying requirement. Even if full reconstruction of the logic that is embedded in existing systems is achieved, recourse to the business and/or first principles is usually required to clarify and confirm these findings to arrive at the definitive correct, consistent, and complete business algorithm.

We can intuit that the business algorithm exists in every enterprise, because we know that enterprises convert raw data into useful outcomes every day. At this point, you may be wondering whether, like Neo in The Matrix, you should take the red pill or the blue pill!

We have been successfully building enterprise scale business algorithms for nearly a decade. This gives us empirical evidence that justifies the red pill – the pill that leads to a new belief system and new ways of solving problems. For instance, a single omnibus algorithm deriving all billing line items from raw clinical data for 42 hospitals and 121 clinics is described in a later chapter of this book[5]; or complete recalculation and remediation of an active $65 billion defined-benefits scheme for a million-member pension fund, right down to adjusting precision as we cross prior legacy systems implementation boundaries during the 35 years the scheme has been operating.

If enterprise scale algorithms are real as described, then the traditional IT approaches to requirements gathering, and systems architecture, design, and development, have just been offered a substantial challenge. Belief in the business algorithm means that we should invert the traditional development approach so that the data and process requirements are derived as dependents of the algorithm rather than the other way around. Our experience is that this can lead to (up to) an order of magnitude improvement in time, cost, and risk to produce equivalent systems.

I recently met with a senior Government figure who has been charged with rebuilding his country's entire welfare payments system, which distributes hundreds of billions of dollars annually. The current environment is spread across more than 200 legacy systems, with no overarching data, process, or rules design apparent during the system's 40 years of evolution. The underlying business algorithm obviously exists because real world data is converted into millions of payments every day, but the algorithm itself is not visible, and the ability to re-collate it must seem far-fetched.

Where would we start? We could acquire and normalize the data across all the systems to give a data centric viewpoint. We could analyse the external events, with their inputs and outputs, to develop a process centric architecture. But in either case, we would still not have the business algorithm, so how would we calculate the entitlements which are the purpose of the system? Furthermore, without the algorithm, we do not have any independent means to validate that these re-derived data or process maps are correct or relevant. At best, we could say that they mirror the legacy environment, but if that is our objective, we haven't advanced much – I am sure the Government will be hoping for more.

However, if we build the business algorithm first and foremost, then we can clearly infer the required data; and when we have defined the data, we can devise optimal processes to support it. These new data and process models are likely to look rather different compared to the legacy influenced maps described by traditional approaches.

We suggested earlier that discovering and re-collating the business algorithm from existing systems can be infeasible, sometimes impossible. However, we have developed techniques and approaches that help mitigate this problem.

---

[5] This use case is the basis for our winning case study in the **Business Rules Excellence Awards 2018** (http://br-excellenceawards.org/)
available on our website
http://idiomsoftware.com/DOCS/Download/d3058f0c-ce4c-4322-8c93-914378f8e178.pdf

BUILDING THE BUSINESS ALGORITHM

The key to building an enterprise-wide algorithm is the *topology*. The topology is a breakdown of the business algorithm into logical units-of-work (which for convenience we have called 'decision models') that allows us to normalize the business logic, the algebra, and the rules within. In this context, 'normalize' means to reduce the algorithm to its simplest form, which requires that it be described using the smallest number of parts, without overlap or redundancy, that is required to achieve the outcomes.

There are several ways to break-down the entire algorithm so that we can address it piecemeal. None can be based on systems, data, or processes, which are artificially derived constructs that do not inherently define the enterprise, and in the context of a new solution, they should not even yet exist (and if they do, we must challenge the basis on which they were created, lest we simply remake the mistakes of the past). Of course, the real-world raw data exists somewhere 'out-there', but we do not yet know which of that data is relevant to the mission of this enterprise – only the algorithm can tell us that.

This is the critical point of this paper (assuming that you have taken the red pill) – if the business logic, algebra, and rules are scattered across the existing system components as properties of data and/or process, then by definition:

- those data and/or process components already exist, rightly or wrongly (and there is no way to empirically assess rightness or wrongness prior to the algorithm, which has been 'lost' by virtue of its scattered, piecemeal implementation); and

- no competing classification scheme for normalizing the business logic, algebra, and rules in the algorithm is plausible, since they are already declared to be properties of the data and/or processes per a) above.

This means that the specification of the business algorithm is compromised by having to adhere to, and to be normalized in accordance with, an artificial topology that is an historical accident at best. And for those with a general knowledge of normalization, having to normalize the internal elements of the algorithm around predefined data and process constructs must constrict and compromise the definition of those elements. Essentially, normalization cannot be achieved around a fixed topology without forcing the meaning of the thing being normalized, potentially leading to redundancy, errors, and omissions. The implication is that this approach is detrimental to the correct normalization and definition of the algorithm, and by extension, of the enterprise itself.

By following the traditional approach, we are implicitly locked into an historical data and process architecture in which the algorithm has neither status nor visibility. And if the data and/or processes already exist, by what means were they discovered and validated without the business algorithm? By definition, the only purpose for both data and processes is to support the algorithm, which is the source of the 'useful outcomes'; without the algorithm, they have no purpose. No system should be collecting and processing data without prior understanding the 'useful outcomes' that are required.

Therefore, we need a new topology. Our new topology concept should precede the definition of data and processes and, will in fact, ultimately define them both. It should be based on existing and fundamental business concepts including:

- The most important is first principles. In our Government payments example, the first principles will be found in legislation and regulations – for instance, we are currently executing decision models that exactly implement key pieces of legislation as described in the chapter on *Payroll Remediation*[6] In financial organisations like banking and insurance, the first principles extend beyond legislation and regulation to include the customer promises and obligations that arise from product disclosure statements, etc.

- The inherent subdivisions of responsibilities and expertise within the enterprise provides another useful dimension, for instance product ownership, financial management, customer management, etc. Each of these subdivisions of enterprise governance should be represented by relevant proxies in the business algorithm.

The four-step algorithm lifecycle is from raw data to useful outcome. This includes inherent and logical subsets of the business algorithm that manage:

1. Data acquisition and validation; do I have enough data of suitable quality for the calculation of the useful outcomes?

2. Transformation into the idiom of the enterprise: The calculation of outcomes is always defined using an idiom that is proprietary to the enterprise, unless it is a commodity business that has no 'haecceity' – that is, no unique characteristics. Perhaps surprisingly, transformation to the idiom is often the major part of the business algorithm's calculation effort.

3. Calculation of the useful outcomes that are the proximate purpose of the business algorithm, and by extension the enterprise itself. This usually means approval for and then value of each specific transaction context (in our Government example, is the person entitled to be paid, and if so, how much? In insurance, this would include underwriting and rating; and/or claims adjudication and payment.)

4. Workflow. What do we do next? New events must be generated to prompt other systems, both internal and external, to respond appropriately to the useful outcomes. These generated events are the responsibility of the algorithm and are required to ensure that the end-state of the entire eco-system is complete, consistent, and correct.

Each of these three major perspectives (including the four lifecycle steps of the algorithm) is an original source of requirements that will only change when the business itself changes at a fundamental level. Each may require us to redirect analysis effort back to existing systems in order to understand the current implementation of the algorithm, so that we do usually end up inspecting legacy systems in detail. However, the legacy implementations are a reflection of somebody else's interpretation of requirements at some earlier point in time. They may be a corroborating source, but they do not fundamentally define the requirements.

If we aim to normalize the algorithm, then we need a classification structure that truly reflects the quiddity and the haecceity of the enterprise, and which will last the test of time. This ideal structure is not based on data or processes, which are artificial and temporal constructs.

---

[6] Deloitte Limited, New Zealand, winning case study in the **Business Rules Excellence Awards 2018** (http://br-excellenceawards.org/)

Each of the major perspectives above are important to constructing a long-term classification structure (i.e. the topology) for the algorithm, and their intersections may give rise to many decision models, so that a complete topology might include tens to hundreds of decision models.

Deriving the specific useful outcomes for any particular transaction will likely require adjudication by many of these decision models within the boundary of the transaction being executed. This gives us an orchestration problem within the overall business algorithm, which we resolve by building a meta (decision) model to manage the orchestration of the many topographical models required.

The net result is that any process that is triggered by an external event simply presents its raw data to the business algorithm for adjudication and conversion into the useful outcomes. Not only does the external process not understand what decision models will process its request, it must not know. If it explicitly requests the execution of specific models, then it presumes an internal knowledge of the business algorithm, which by definition means it has ceased to be a business only artefact – it is now inextricably bound to the process implementation.

Furthermore, that process should not be aware of the 'useful outcomes' that will be produced, nor by extension, what subsequent process those useful outcomes will trigger. Both of these will be driven by the algorithm, which will determine which outcomes are needed, and what processing instructions those outcomes require to drive the broader eco-system.

For the sake of clarity, we are proposing that all business logic, algebra, and rules can be defined into the business algorithm, on a fully normalized basis so that there is only ever one representation of any logical requirement within the business algorithm, and the algorithm in aggregate is complete, consistent, and correct across the enterprise.

THE ALGORITHM IN OPERATION

However, this is not to be confused with *implementation* – the entire algorithm, and many distinct subsets of it – can be deployed into multiple execution locations so that it can run 'in process' wherever it may be required. This allows for fast execution.

In our own case, this is usually achieved by generating the decision models into code and loading the individual decision model executables (dll's, JARs) into the database. Any process location (back-end processes, web servers, centralised services, etc.) can access the algorithm's public interface ('in process', via a connector, REST service, etc.), which then loads and caches the executables as required from the database.

The relevant set of models required for any particular location is dynamically defined by the nature of the transactions that are visible at that location – it does not need to be pre-defined. It does not usually include all decision models that comprise the business algorithm. This approach is currently being upgraded to utilise more recent deployment strategies including containerization (Docker, cri-o, Heroku, AWS Lambda, microservices, etc.).

We normally expect <10 milliseconds for standard calls to the algorithm, but some extreme cases that process large amounts of data inside the transaction can extend this by an order of magnitude or more.

What is a large amount of data for a single transaction? Anywhere from 1million-10million data nodes. Anything less than 1million data nodes per transaction is considered business as usual. At 10million nodes, we suggest a change in approach to the definition of transactions.

To get some sense of the scale of the decision models and algorithms that we are talking about, and of the set that may be distributed: Our largest single decision model (the defined benefit calculation mentioned earlier) is implemented by ~300,000 lines of code (Java and/or C#); our largest set of decision models executed in a single request is several dozen; and our largest business algorithm has ~100 decision models in the enterprise wide set, so that the complete business algorithm for an enterprise can easily extend to millions of lines of code.

CONCLUSION

The above discussion describes an approach that captures the *quiddity* and the *haecceity* of each unique enterprise by capturing its own particular 'business algorithm'.

Of great importance, the business logic, algebra, and rules in this algorithm must be normalized (similar to how we normalize data to get a sound data design). Managing and navigating this normalization process requires a topology that is derived from the enterprise's inherent structures. This specifically excludes *systems* – the business algorithm is captured and normalized independently of systems considerations to ensure that it is not contaminated by artificial or historical technology or methodology constraints. And in an inversion of current practice, the business algorithm can then be used to re-derive both data and processes from the first principles that are provided by the algorithm. This approach can reduce time cost and risk to develop systems by substantial margins.

Evaluation of Patient Eligibility for Publicly-Funded Vaccines[1]

David Lyalin and Warren Williams (*retired*)
Centers for Disease Control and Prevention (CDC[2]), USA

BACKGROUND

There are federal, state, and local government immunization programs in the United States that provide publicly-funded vaccines to eligible patients. The largest of these programs is a federally-funded Vaccines for Children (VFC) program (CDC 2016). It is implemented by the Centers for Disease Control and Prevention (CDC) and state health departments (recipients of VFC funds). Participating healthcare providers determine each patient's eligibility for a needed vaccine, administer publicly- and privately-funded vaccine doses as appropriate, and report vaccination events and eligibility status back to immunization programs.

Immunization Information Systems (IIS) (CDC 2019) help immunization programs collect and aggregate patients' eligibility information from healthcare providers. Ultimately, that eligibility information supports two objectives: 1) ensure that publicly-funded vaccines are administered only to eligible patients and 2) support vaccines' accountability measures.

This chapter discusses a case study that applies business rules and decision table techniques to document recommendations for evaluating a patient's eligibility for publicly-funded immunization programs and private coverage.

CONTEXT MODEL — PROCESS DIAGRAM

Figure 1 shows a simplified process diagram depicting responsibilities of the main parties involved in evaluating a patient's eligibility for publicly-funded vaccines in context of the immunization domain.

- Immunization Program, shown at the bottom, provides publicly-funded vaccines to participating Healthcare Providers.
- Healthcare Providers, shown at the top, determine a patient's vaccination needs, screen patients to assign the appropriate eligibility/coverage category, administer publicly-funded vaccine doses if appropriate, and report vaccination events and eligibilities back to the immunization programs.
- Immunization Information Systems (IIS), shown in the middle, collect and aggregate vaccination and eligibility information from healthcare providers about vaccine doses spent (i.e., doses administered, wasted, spoiled/expired, etc.). An IIS uses that information to support accountability requirements of its immunization program and reporting needs of healthcare providers.

---

[1] This chapter is based on the article "How Business Rules and Decision Tables Support Evaluation of Patient Eligibility for Publicly-Funded Vaccines" in the Business Rules Journal, Vol. 14, No. 9,(Sep. 2013). URL: http://www.brcommunity.com/b716.php

[2] The findings and conclusions in this publication are those of the authors and do not necessarily represent the official position of the Centers for Disease Control and Prevention.

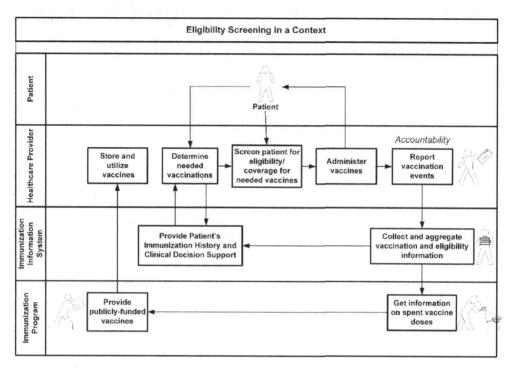

Figure 1. Evaluating a patient's eligibility/coverage for needed vaccines in context of the immunization domain.

DOMAIN MODEL — BUSINESS VOCABULARY

Terms and definitions for this project have been captured in a domain model (Figure 2). Following are a few excerpts from the business vocabulary that will be used in this article:

- Eligibility — describes an association of a patient with a public immunization program, e.g., patient is eligible for the Vaccines for Children (VFC) program
- Coverage — describes an association of a patient with a private insurance or out-of-pocket pay, e.g., patient is covered by the private insurance
- Eligibility/Coverage Categories
  - o VFC program — Medicaid
  - o VFC program — American Indian and Alaska Native
  - o VFC program — Uninsured
  - o VFC program — Underinsured (i.e., patient has private health insurance, but it does not cover needed vaccines — for example, because insurance caps vaccine coverage at a certain amount)
  - o State program — Eligible (various degree of granularity, state-specific)
  - o Private coverage — Covered (private insurance or out-of-pocket pay) = VFC Ineligible

For a single vaccination event, a patient may be eligible for the VFC program, and for a state immunization program, and (s)he might have private insurance coverage. So, the patient's eligibility/coverage for a needed vaccine dose should be selected from a pool of available eligibilities and coverages.

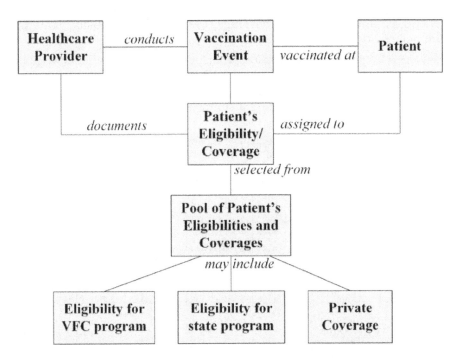

Figure 2. A fragment of the domain diagram for evaluating a patient's eligibility/coverage for needed vaccines

DECISION MODEL — ELIGIBILITY SCREENING CONDITIONS

Various considerations are involved when screening a patient for eligibility for public vaccines. Those considerations are very different in nature — from age, to race, to state immunization policies, and to a type of healthcare provider. Typical considerations in determining eligibility include:

- Patient's age (i.e., has patient reached 19th birthday?)
- Does patient have Medicaid (publicly-funded health insurance)?
- Is patient American Indian or Alaska Native?
- Does patient have private health insurance? If so:
  - o Does this private health insurance cover a needed vaccine?
  - o Has the private insurance vaccines-coverage cap been reached?
- Is healthcare provider of a qualified type (i.e., Federally Qualified Health Center (FQHC) or Rural Health Clinic (RHC))?
- Does state provide publicly-funded vaccines in addition to the federal VFC program?
- Does patient meet State immunization program's eligibility requirements?

On practice, these considerations can be combined in intricate combinations of multiple conditions that reflect immunization programs' policy and requirements. Decision tables and business rules were logical choices of instruments to analyze and sort out all of these aspects of the eligibility screening. Following are two guiding business rules formulated by a panel of immunization experts:

- Single eligibility/coverage should be assigned to a patient for every vaccination event/dose administered.

- Recommended hierarchy of choices for a patient's eligibility/coverage, in general, is: private insurance coverage, VFC program eligibility, State program eligibility.

Figure 3 depicts a fragment of the decision table for evaluating a patient's eligibility status. The initial version of this decision table had been developed during an in-person facilitated meeting of twelve immunization experts. It includes all conditions that were discussed above, documenting a comprehensive set of eligibility screening scenarios.

Abbreviations: "Y" = Yes, "N" = No, dash "-" means that it does not matter for the outcome of a scenario if it is "Y" or "N", "X" points to actions that should be taken for this scenario, and blank indicates actions that are not applicable for this scenario.

SCENARIOS Numbers	1	2	3	4	5	6	7	8		21	22	23	24	25	26
Partitioned Table 1 Reference	1	4	4	4	4	4	2	3		7	7	7	7	na	na
Partitioned Table 2 Reference	na	9	9	6	13	12	na	9		3	4	4	5	na	na
Partitioned Table 3 Reference	na	na	na	na	na	na	na	na		na	3	1	na	1	2,3
CONDITIONS															
Reached 19th birthday: Y/N	N	N	N	N	N	N	N	N		N	N	N	N	Y	Y
Medicaid: Y/N	Y	Y	Y	Y	Y	Y	Y	Y		N	N	N	N	-	-
American Indian or Alaska Native: Y/N	N	N	N	N	N	N	Y	Y		N	N	N	N	-	-
Patient has private health insurance: Y/N	N	Y	Y	Y	Y	Y	N	Y		Y	Y	Y	Y	-	-
Private insurance covers needed Vaccine: Y/N	-	Y	Y	N	Y	Y	-	Y		Y	Y	Y	Y	-	-
Private insurance Vaccine cap reached: Y/N	-	Y	Y	-	N	N	-	Y		Y	Y	N	N	-	-
Patient at Provider Organization (Facility) Type: (R)HC or (F)QHC or (D)elegated Authority	-	N	Y	-	N	N	-	N		Y	N	N	-	-	-
Choose to use VFC: Y/N	-	-	-	-	Y	N	-	-		-	-	-	-	-	-
State policy: VFC & Underinsured, or VFC & Underinsured Select, or Universal, or Universal Select State, or Other – meaning not VFC Only: Y/N	-	-	-	-	-	-	-	-		-	N	Y	-	-	-
Meets Grantee Program eligibility criteria: Y/N	-	-	-	-	-	-	-	-		-	-	Y	-	Y	N
ACTIONS															
General VFC Eligibility Status															
1. Record Patient VFC eligible	X	X	X	X	X		X	X		X					
2. Record Patient VFC ineligible (or Private coverage)						X					X	X	X	X	X
VFC Eligibility Criteria															
3. Check "Medicaid"	X	X	X	X	X		X	X							
4. Check "American Indian or Alaska Native"							X	X							
5. Check "Uninsured"															
6. Check "Underinsured"										X					
General Grantee (State) Eligibility Status															
7. Record Patient Grantee Program eligible												X		X	
8. Record Patient Grantee Program ineligible											X				X

Figure 3. A fragment of the decision table for evaluating a patient's eligibility/coverage for needed vaccines

Obviously, this decision table is big and, with added detailed conditions for state immunization programs, can quickly grow to be much larger in terms of size and complexity. And that is why we turned to the partitioning idea and approach.

DECISION MODEL — PARTITIONED VERSION

Partitioning is an established engineering approach to address complexity. A model of the complex business system gets dissected into more 'digestible' parts, allowing a practitioner to analyze each part separately and improve comprehension of the entire business.

Accordingly, the initial, large decision table has been partitioned into three smaller tables, which are associated with three logical processes on the process model (Figure 4):

Decision tables support and provide logic for Patient screening

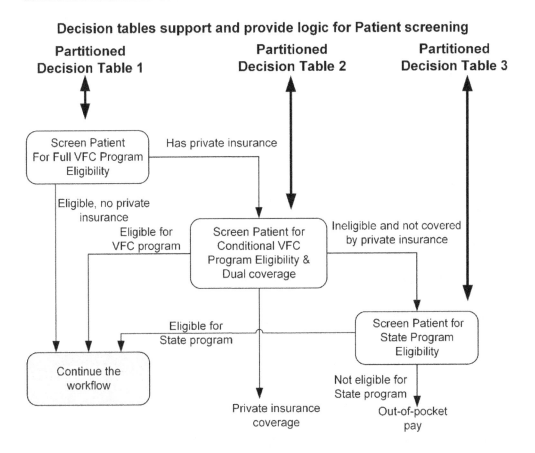

Figure 4. Partitioned decision tables and process steps

1. Screen patient for full VFC program eligibility (decision table is presented in Figure 5). Patients who have Medicaid, are American Indians or Alaska Native, or are totally uninsured are fully eligible for all VFC program vaccines. This represents the most common, simplest case.

	SCENARIOS							
	1	2	3	4	5	6	7	8
Reference to complete Decision Table	1	7	8,9	2-6	10	11-16	18-24	17
Reference to partitioned Decision Table 2	na	na	9	6,9, 12,13	na	7,8, 10-13	1–5	na
CONDITIONS:								
Medicaid: Y/N	Y	Y	Y	Y	N	N	N	N
American Indian or Alaska Native: Y/N	N	Y	Y	N	Y	Y	N	N
Patient has private health insurance: Y/N	N	N	Y	Y	N	Y	Y	N
ACTIONS:								
General VFC Eligibility Status								
1. Record Patient VFC eligible for all program Vaccines	X	X	X	X	X	X		X
2. Further assess Patient's private insurance coverage - see Decision Table 2			X	X		X	X	
VFC Eligibility Criteria								
3. Record "Medicaid"	X	X	X	X				
4. Record "American Indian or Alaska Native"		X	X		X	X		
5. Record "Uninsured"					X			X

Figure 5. Partitioned decision table 1

2. Screen patient for conditional VFC program eligibility and dual-coverage (decision table is presented in Figure 6). This process includes patients who have private insurance. Outcome depends on such factors as whether the specific vaccine needed is covered by the patient's insurance, whether the patient's insurance vaccine cap has been reached, and the type of provider (i.e., FQHC or RHC).

As a result of the patient's screening for the conditional VFC eligibility, one of the three outcomes can emerge: 1) patient is VFC-eligible for a specific vaccine, 2) patient is covered by a private insurance for a specific vaccine, or 3) patient is VFC-ineligible for the needed vaccine and private insurance doesn't cover it. The first two outcomes signify the end of the patient's screening process.

The third outcome leads to an additional step — patient's screening for State program eligibility.

					SCENARIOS						
	1	**2**	**3**	**4**	**5**	**6**	**7**	**8**	**9**		**13**
Reference to complete Decision Table	18	19	21	22, 23	24	4	15	16	2, 3, 8, 9		6, 13
Reference to partitioned Decision Table 1	7	7	7	7	7	4	6	6	3, 4		4, 6
Reference to partitioned Decision Table 3	na	1-3	na	1-3	na	na	na	na	na		na
CONDITIONS:											
Private insurance covers needed Vaccine: Y/N **	N	N	Y	Y	Y	N	N	N	Y		Y
Private insurance Vaccine cap reached: Y/N	-	-	Y	Y	N	-	-	-	Y		N
Patient at appropriate Provider Organization type: Y/N ● RHC or FQHC or Delegated Authority	Y	N	Y	N	-	-	Y	N	-		-
Already has VFC eligibility (AI/AN and/or Medicaid): Y/N	N	N	N	N	N	Y	Y	Y	Y		Y
Patient has Medicaid: Y/N	–	-	-	-	-	Y	N	N	Y		-
Choose to use private insurance: Y/N	-	-	-	-	-	-	-	-	-		N
ACTIONS:											
General VFC Eligibility Status											
1. Record Patient VFC eligible for specific Vaccine	X		X								
2. Record Patient VFC ineligible		X		X	X						
3. Change VFC status to ineligible											
VFC Eligibility Criteria											
4. Record "Underinsured"	X		X				X				
VFC Eligibility Reason											
5. Record insurance Vaccine cap reached		X									
6. Record insurance does not cover needed Vaccine	X						X				
VFC Ineligibility Reason											
7. Record Vaccine covered by private ins (sole coverage)					X						
8. Record not at appropriate type of Provider Organization		X		X							
9. Record choose to use private ins (dual coverage)											
Other											
10. No further action						X		X	X		X
11. Evaluate Patient for Grantee Program eligibility		X		X							

Figure 6. Partitioned decision table 2

3. Screen patient for State program eligibility (decision table is presented in Figure 7). Each State would detail out the eligibility criteria for their specific immunization program. If the patient is determined ineligible for the State program (or if there is no State program), then he/she would have to pay out-of-pocket for the vaccine.

	SCENARIOS		
	1	**2**	**3**
Reference to complete Decision Table	20,23,25	26	19,22,26
Reference to partitioned Decision Table 2	2,4	2,4	2,4
CONDITIONS:			
Are you one of these VFC State Vaccine purchasing policies? (VFC & Underinsured , or VFC & Underinsured Select, or Universal, or Universal Select State, or Other – meaning not VFC Only) In other words, does your State have a Vaccine purchase policy in addition to VFC?	Y	Y	N
Meets Grantee Program criteria: Y/N	Y	N	-
ACTIONS:			
General Grantee (State) Eligibility Status			
1. Record Patient Grantee Program eligible	X		
2. Record Patient Grantee Program ineligible		X	X
Grantee Eligibility Criteria			
Record ... <to be developed by each Grantee>			

Figure 7. Partitioned decision table 3

This process sequence of the patient's eligibility screening (presented in Figure 4) does not create a comprehensive pool of the patient's eligibilities and coverages to select from, but rather presents a logical order of steps to determine which eligibility/coverage to use. For a given vaccine encounter, if a patient has been found to be 'fully' eligible for all VFC program vaccines, then there is no need to rescreen the patient for each vaccine needed.

However, if a patient is not 'fully' eligible, then the patient needs the 'conditional' screening for each vaccine to determine if the patient's insurance covers the vaccine or not. In cases when the patient has full or conditional VFC Eligibility, no screening for the State program eligibility would be conducted. This reflects the hierarchy described above, advising that State program funds should be used only in cases when the patient is not eligible for the VFC program and does not have private insurance coverage.

UNEXPECTED OBSTACLE — FACTOR OF PEOPLE'S PERCEPTION

So, now instead of the one large table there are three smaller ones, logically connected via the associated process steps. It appeared to be a sound solution, but subject matter experts (SMEs) had difficulty using the partitioned tables, especially to trace a single operational scenario through three partitioned tables. Using the three-step process to determine eligibility turned out to be more challenging than getting it from a single pool of eligibilities and coverages.

Additional illustrations and numbering schemes that link scenarios in decision tables together did not substantially help SMEs navigate these tables. We ended up going back to the original 'all-inclusive' decision table (shown in Figure 3) and placed partitioned tables (shown in Figures 5-7) in the appendix of the recommendations document.

CONCLUSION

Decomposition is a fine and a proven technique, but it can cause problems. In this case, the partitioning of a large, 'all-inclusive' decision table into more manageable, smaller decision tables, while being conceptually sound, led to a prescriptive set of associated process steps and resulted in challenges of acceptance by SMEs and users. Such an outcome when using the decomposition approach is in line with experience of other practitioners. For example, Alec Sharp in his 2011 workshop *From Process Redesign to IT Requirements*, stated that "Carving up a single process into multiple, one-page diagrams (effectively, a decomposition) can destroy the story." Lesson learned: a logically sound and elegant solution is not always the most practicable one.

In spite of that decomposition-related disappointment, the overall outcome of implementing the decision tables and business rules techniques in our public health settings resulted in a positive outcome. The recommendations we developed (AIRA 2011) are used by many immunization information systems in the United States (Williams et al.).

ACKNOWLEDGEMENTS

Authors would like to acknowledge:

- Our colleagues from state immunization information systems, state immunization programs, Vaccines for Children (VFC) program, software vendors, and public health consultants who volunteered to participate in the experts' panel and contributed greatly to the development of recommendations and logic for evaluating a patient's eligibility.

- Team from Advanced Strategies, Inc., especially Gail DeCosta who developed initial version of decision tables during the facilitated meeting of immunization subject matter experts.

REFERENCES

(CDC 2016) Vaccines for Children Program, URL: http://www.cdc.gov/vaccines/programs/vfc/index.html

(CDC 2019) Immunization Information Systems, URL: http://www.cdc.gov/vaccines/programs/iis/about.html

(AIRA 2011) AIRA Modeling of Immunization Registry Operations Work Group (Eds). Immunization Information System Collaboration with Vaccines For Children Program and Grantee Immunization Programs. Atlanta, GA: American Immunization Registry Association. April, 2011. URL: https://repository.immregistries.org/resource/immunization-information-system-collaboration-with-vaccines-for-children-program-and-grantee-immuniz-1/from/AIRA-products-and-activities/best-practices/MIROW-guides/

(Williams et al.) Williams W, Lowery E, Lyalin D, Lambrecht N, Riddick S, Sutliff C, Papadouka V. "Development and Utilization of Best Practice Operational Guidelines for Immunization Information Systems." Journal of Public Health Management and Practice. 2011; 17(5): 449-456.

Section 2

Business Rules:
Execution

A California Bank, USA
Nominated by OpenRules, Inc., USA

1. EXECUTIVE SUMMARY / ABSTRACT

This case study describes a successful implementation of business rules within a large California bank[1] with 80 billion in assets. The bank needed to modernize the existing onboarding system by adding over 600 new, dynamically-formulated KYC (Know Your Customer) questions. The new interaction logic was very complex, requiring the complicated UI to be dynamically modified for different types of customers, accounts, and planned account activities. The questions to be asked were dependent on previously-provided answers and already-known information about customers and their accounts. Hard-coding of such interaction logic into the existing onboarding system would be both cost- and time-prohibitive. Instead, a radically new approach driven by externalized rules was implemented to significantly reduce implementation and maintenance costs as well as delivery timelines.

To add new capabilities and seamlessly extend the old system to match the existing User Experience a new, rules-based system became a necessity. The bank evaluated several business rules frameworks including major commercial and open source products and selected the one that best matched the bank's needs. As a result, the new system was successfully developed, tested, and deployed on the bank's production servers using rules-based web services. The new system addressed the core challenges and saved an otherwise failing project allowing the bank to meet regulatory commitments and deadlines.

The rules-based approach allowed the bank to:
  (1) catch up on all time lost and still deliver on time;
  (2) integrate the new system with the existing IT infrastructure and to provide seamless user experience and
  (3) create an organizational environment where Business and IT worked together as one team with a minimal learning curve.

Along with essential cost and time savings, the bank listed the following benefits:
  * very powerful yet intuitive rules and template architecture;
  * short run/test cycles of building dynamic web applications;
  * all rules defined declaratively, externalized out of the application code and can be understood and modified by new personal.

Now, the bank uses the same business rules framework for another mission-critical application related to risk management.

2. OVERVIEW

This case study describes a successful implementation of business rules within one of the largest California's banks for a highly dynamic web application that supports complex customer account management processes.

---

[1] The financial institution requested anonymity

The bank has more than 6,000 business users working in branches creating new and modifying existing customer accounts. The existing onboarding system was in production for years and used a traditional (not rules-based) GUI technology. To comply with regulatory requirements, the bank needed to revamp their onboarding process by incorporating over 600 new, dynamically displayed questions and sections to complete KYC requirements for different types of customers and accounts that were being on-boarded.

The bank faced major technical and organizational challenges. The interaction logic was very complex requiring the graphical views to be dynamically modified for different types of customers, accounts, and planned account activities. The questions to be asked were dependent on previously-provided answers and already known information about customers and their accounts. If such interaction logic was hard-coded again, then delivery of such a system (due to bugs and potential QA issues) and future maintenance costs would be time- and cost-prohibitive. So, the bank started to consider a rules-based approach that would allow externalizing the logic in the form of user-friendly business rules that could drive both interaction and composition of the user interfaces.

Another challenge that the team had to solve was a seamless integration with the existing onboarding solution for users. Specifically, the requirement was to have end users not to be aware that they are leaving their existing application from beginning to end of the onboarding process. That required matching the existing UI experience and providing a seamless integration between the old and new systems.

In the face of encountered difficulties with no solutions available on the one hand, and looming regulatory fines, on the other hand, the bank had to drastically rethink and seek for a solution that could still work. They opted for a solution that could utilize an off-the-shelf rules-based framework to meet complexity of the requirements. As a result, the new system was developed, tested, and deployed on the bank's production servers using rules-based web application and web services frameworks.

The selected rules-based approach allowed the banks' business analysts and software developers to work as one team by adding new functionality and validating all combinations of questions/answers to identify any inconsistencies and flag them to meet strict regulatory and compliance requirements. As a result, the developed system proved to be very successful: (1) bank was able to save approximately six months as the result of the pivot and therefore met the originally committed timelines; (2) the system was developed in-house with very little external professional help which reduced budget three times by saving on extensive customizations that would have been required to a vendor-based solutions.

3. BUSINESS CONTEXT

Prior to this implementation, the existing onboarding system was in production for years and used a traditional (not rules-based) GUI technology to support more than 6,000 business users working concurrently on creating new and modifying existing customer accounts. The existing system was quite efficient, but the entire interaction and presentation logic was hard-coded, controlled by experienced programmers, and it was difficult to make any changes. To comply with new KYC (Know Your Customer) regulations and address them for each of their unique channels - each servicing quite diverse customer types. It was necessary to implement complex, dynamic flows with overlaying UI interactions including different operating modes, new complex rules which drive system behavior in response to many of the customer types, user actions, ability to pause, save, resume, restore, or cancel different branches of the dialogs, hard stops, etc. The bank needed to add over 600 new, dynamically formulated questions depending on customer or account types, planned account activities and previously provided answers. The existing solution was not able to accommodate new requirements neither in time for delivery timelines nor from the cost perspective. A new approach – using rules to drive the complexity and reduce the cost of development became the only viable option.

4. THE KEY INNOVATIONS

4.1 Innovative Solution

The bank quickly understood that applying the traditional business rules approach "as is" was not going to be successful either. To solve the business issues described above, it was not enough to use generic decision tables and other traditional forms of business rules. To create a new, rules-based graphical interface with a very complex interaction and presentation logic, the bank needed a business rule platform that already provided a rich set of the predefined rules for building (1) web-based layout templates and (2) rules-based GUI navigation. The bank found an open source platform which provided such functionality out of the box without requiring a long learning curve. The new BR platform supported the integrated use of the rule engine and rendering engine that became the foundation for the successful and quick implementation. The following capabilities essentially simplified the development of the required functionality:

- The predefined rule templates already dealt with such GUI concepts as pages, sections, and various types of questions that could be used to easily configured dynamic web pages. The new product already included page navigation and updating rule templates which become critical for the implementation of the new interaction logic. The predefined decision tables for building dynamic dialogs allowed the bank specialists to naturally represent such pieces of the interaction logic as: *if the answer to a question "A" is X and the answer to the question "B" contains Y and Z, then hide the question "C" and display the multi-choice question "D" with the possible values V1, V2, and V3*
- Below is an example of an Excel-based decision table with interaction rules that allow a user to define how the dynamic content should be modified in real time based on the user answers:

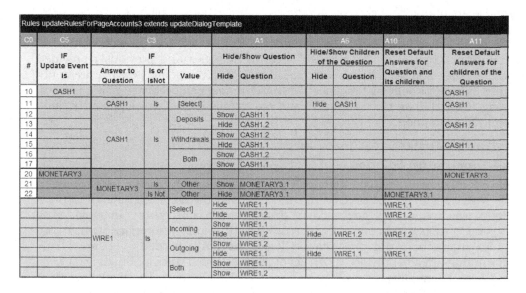

#	IF Update Event is	IF Answer to Question	Is or IsNot	Value	Hide/Show Question Hide	Question	Hide/Show Children of the Question Hide	Question	Reset Default Answers for Question and its children	Reset Default Answers for children of the Question
10	CASH1									CASH1
11		CASH1	Is	[Select]			Hide	CASH1		CASH1
12				Deposits	Show	CASH1.1				
13					Hide	CASH1.2				CASH1.2
14		CASH1	Is	Withdrawals	Show	CASH1.2				
15					Hide	CASH1.1				CASH1.1
16				Both	Show	CASH1.2				
17					Show	CASH1.1				
20	MONETARY3									MONETARY3
21		MONETARY3	Is	Other	Show	MONETARY3.1				
22			Is Not	Other	Hide	MONETARY3.1			MONETARY3.1	
				[Select]	Hide	WIRE1.1			WIRE1.1	
					Hide	WIRE1.2			WIRE1.2	
		WIRE1	Is	Incoming	Show	WIRE1.1				
					Hide	WIRE1.2	Hide	WIRE1.2	WIRE1.2	
				Outgoing	Show	WIRE1.2				
					Hide	WIRE1.1	Hide	WIRE1.1	WIRE1.1	
				Both	Show	WIRE1.1				
					Show	WIRE1.2				

And here is an example of a typical dialog with dynamically modified content:

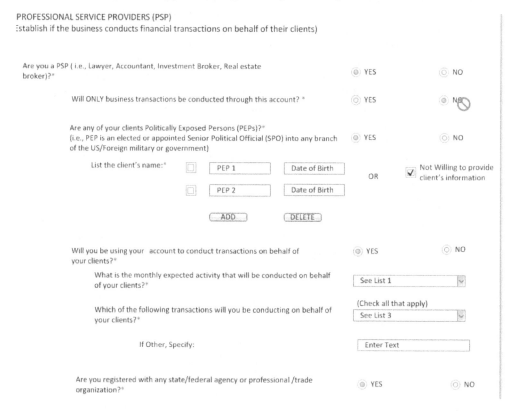

- Using this type of business rules, it was easy to extend and customize the provided rule templates when the interaction logic specific for this application required adding new types of rules
- The provided templates for web forms allowed the bank to present the major graphical components required by this web application. However, to

support the same look and feel as the old GUI, the bank needed to customize and to extend the provided representations for different types of pages, sections, and questions. It became a relatively simple task to add custom CSS, HTML, and JavaScript directly to decision and layout tables presented in Excel and supported by the selected business rules product

- The supported Java API and web service deployment capabilities allowed a quick and simple integration of the rule and rendering engines with existing system including its data warehousing system, ESB (enterprise service bus) and the application server

- The new rules-based approach essentially improved integration across business areas by bringing together business people, developers, QA, and management. It allowed business analysts and developers to work together as one team by not only specifying new rules and web forms, but representing them in Excel tables, creating and running tests, visualizing the resulting GUI, and iteratively improving the integrated system

- The new approach essentially improved the flexibility of decision making and expedite the development and testing processes.

4.2 Impact and Implementation

The new rules-based approach had positive impact on the bank's employees giving them the common goals and tools to achieve them. Previously business people specified what to do and written specifications were given to developers for implementation. Then the implemented software was given to QA engineers for testing. With a new approach, all these three categories of employees were combined in one team constantly working together under the same highly challenging deadline.

The rules-based approach provided the following implementation advantages:
- Instead of creating intermediate specifications the team gradually implemented new pages, sections, and questions using rules and layout tables in Excel, which were intuitive enough to be understood by all involved specialists

- The important part of this development approach was the use on the centralized business glossary that provided terminology, uniquely named decision variables and business concepts common for business and technical people

- The test cases prepared by business specialists in Excel became an essential part of the rule repository maintained along with the rules to support future modifications

- As a result, the team (BA+DEV+QA) added new functionality feature-by-feature following immediate testing, correction, and integration. Even the managers could see control development and testing progress every day as new functionality being added and available to all involved people all the time.

4.3 Business and Operational Impact

This successful implementation of advanced business rules and decision concepts demonstrated the advantages of the selected approach. As a result, the new system was developed in time within the dramatically reduced budget. According to the bank, business and operational impact include:
- Increased revenues: while we do not have hard numbers, but the newly introduced business rules framework has much smaller and simpler

licensing requirements and allowed the bank to minimize a number of involved consultants
- Establishment of compliance capabilities in accordance with the government regulations
- Improved maintenance and transparency of business rules or decisions used
- Better synchronized system development and maintenance work of different categories of the bank's employees and consultants from subject matter experts, to developers and QA
- Ease of learning the system implementation by new staff members.

The best proof of the positive impact is the fact that after successfully putting a new onboarding system in production, the bank now uses the same business rules framework and a similar development approach for another mission-critical application related to risk management.

5. HURDLES OVERCOME

The bank faced the following challenges:
- The old system was not able to support new functional requirements
- An immovable delivery deadline as the bank was facing regulatory sanctions if the new features are not delivered on time
- The bank also needed to take into account a lead time for development of training materials and provide necessary training in thousands of branches that required to minimize necessary changes in the user experience.
- Complexity of the interaction logic would make writing the exact specification of new features a lengthy process. The alternative process allowed business analysts to be directly involved in the rules-based development and testing and reducing SDLC time.

With the new rules-based approach, the last challenge was converted to an essential advantage allowing business people to work in concert with developers to dramatically speed-up development and testing processes for new business rules and graphical components.

6. BENEFITS

The key benefits of the new, rules-based approach were based on two major factors:
- It provided off-the-shelf business rules and decision management framework that already included predefined templates for complex interaction rules and web forms framework which could be easily customized
- It incentivized the bank to combine business analysts, developers and testers in one team working together by gradually adding new functionality without the necessity to create intermediate specification documents.

6.1 Cost Savings / Time Reductions

The new business rules platform licensing fees are many times less to compare with the existing platform that caused an essential cost saving for the bank.

The selected approach reduced time-to-market twice by six months (twice less) and essentially simplified specification-implementation-testing cycle allowing the bank to meet a challenging deadline.

6.2 Quality Improvements

The newly-developed system not only added a new required functionality but improved the quality of the solution by making it easier to modify, extend, and to learn for new employees. All of the UI logic was documented in a simple and intuitive, Excel based decision tables like the one shown above.

7. BEST PRACTICES, LEARNING POINTS AND PITFALLS

7.1 Best Practices and Learning Points

✓ Externalized, rules driven UI logic, was easier to document, develop and test
✓ Minimized documentation while improved communication and collaboration Business specialists and developers working in concert.

7.2 Pitfalls

✗ Don't try to develop a rules-based product in house and investigate and compare different off-the-shelf business rules platforms using a clearly defined POC

✗ General-purpose business rules platforms usually require the development of rules repositories from scratch. Find a platform that already supports domain-specific templates and rules repositories with an ability to be extended and customized.

8. COMPETITIVE ADVANTAGES

The bank originally implemented the approach only for its Retail Channel. Other channels used different platforms. By switching to a rules-based approach and by selecting the right business rules platform allowed the Retail channel to complete the delivery of the KYC requirements in time in its complete scope and without any performance or quality issues compared to other internal channels.

9. TECHNOLOGY

The following picture describes the underlying technology infrastructure:

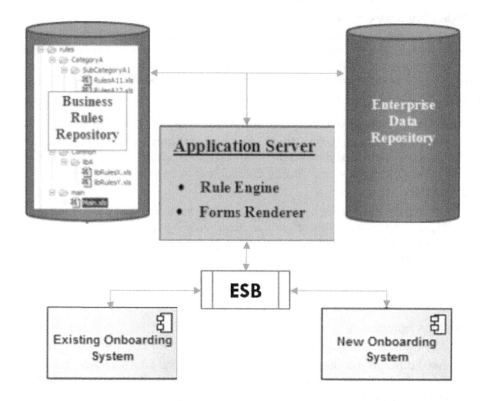

This architecture allowed the existing and new onboarding systems to co-exist (at least initially) and to exchange the customer's data because they share the same Enterprise Data Repository and Enterprise Service Bus (ESB).

10. THE TECHNOLOGY AND SERVICE PROVIDERS

To develop a new on-boarding system, the bank selected OpenRules®, an open source Business Rules and Decision Management system (http://openrules.com). It comes with a built-in component, called "OpenRules Dialog" that was specifically designed for building dynamic web-based questionnaires. The predefined and easily customizable templates for interaction rules and for page, section, and question layouts played the key role in the success of this development. The bank also utilized OpenRules consulting, training, and technical support services.

OpenRules fulfilled the bank's needs with a quickly-completed POC to prove the ability to meet the business requirements; positive reference check; straight-forward Excel-based UI for creation and maintenance of business rules and graphical forms; simple rules configuration logic with predefined and extendable rule templates; minimal learning curve; simple licensing requirements; low cost and a quick development schedule; very responsive technical support.

Deloitte Limited, New Zealand
Nominated by IDIOM Limited, New Zealand

1. EXECUTIVE SUMMARY / ABSTRACT

Deloitte Limited (New Zealand) provides professional services including payroll remediation services to clients throughout New Zealand. NZ enacted complex holiday and termination payment rules in the Holidays Act 2003 that payroll systems have generally failed to implement correctly. The law requires remediation for the last six-years of payroll.

Deloitte developed a rules-based approach to validate, transform, recalculate, and remediate complex payrolls over the full six-year period. The rules are continuously adapted and used by Deloitte consultants throughout the approach, which was first applied to the NZ Police payroll remediation, resulting in a payout exceeding $NZD40m to 20,000staff.

Deloitte has so far remediated the payrolls for more than 20 employers across the country (both public and private), hundreds of thousands of employees, and eight underlying payroll platforms.

This submission describes how Deloitte's use of rules has given it an agile and cost-effective process to recalculate and remediate payroll systems at scale. The NZ Police case is used as a reference case to highlight key elements of the solution described herein.

2. OVERVIEW

Deloitte Limited (New Zealand) [Deloitte] provides professional services including payroll consultancy services to Government and private sector clients throughout NZ.

Payroll systems have attracted global attention for their complexity and scale, with Canada's Phoenix project and the Government of Queensland's Health Department payroll providing examples of what can go wrong.

In 2003, the NZ Government enacted complex holiday and termination payment rules in the 'Holidays Act (2003)' [the Act] that payroll systems have generally failed to implement correctly - Deloitte estimates that up to 80 percent of the country's payrolls are not compliant. The law has recently been strengthened with increase regulatory powers and substantial civil penalties. Errant employers are required by the Act to remediate the last six-years of payroll, with several enforceable actions already issued.

The main issue with compliance with the Holidays Act is that most payroll systems are based on hours (i.e. hours * rate) whereas the Holidays Act is written around days and weeks.

The essence of the act is that when an employee takes a public or annual leave holiday, or any cash equivalent in termination or other special pays, then they should get the same pay as they would have if they had worked that specific day. The Act requires a calculation of the proximate daily pays for the preceding four weeks, and for the preceding year – the correct holiday pay rate is the greater average of these. This is an easy calculation for regular 40 hours per week employees but when overtime, commission, and variable day pattern rosters are considered, it becomes very difficult to configure a traditional COTS payroll system to comply with the Act.

In 2014, Deloitte was approached by NZ Police to review and remediate the NZ police payroll to ensure compliance with the Act. This was one of the earliest-known examples of non-compliance, which has since been found to be widespread.

Deloitte realized that a rules initiative was required and approached a local rules tool vendor for support. Together, Deloitte and the vendor developed an approach to build rules that audit, validate, transform, recalculate, and remediate complex payrolls over the full six-year period, with an additional year for the prior 12-month daily average.

The process has since been made more reusable by building a separate decision model of the underlying Holidays Act legislation, and then using targeted decision models to transform customer specific payroll data for use by the generic Holidays Act model. These models continue to evolve, progressively codifying the expertise that is being built up through multiple customer engagements.

Deloitte has so far remediated the payrolls for over 20 employers across the country (both public and private), hundreds of thousands of employees, and eight underlying payroll vendor platforms.

This process is continuously optimized by codifying the knowledge gained from each engagement into the rules, to the point that eight payrolls are now being remediated in parallel using the same number of staffs as for the first remediation.

During the remediation process, Payroll systems are often found to have systemic inaccuracies, which require rules-based correction before complete recalculation of the payroll can be attempted. Sometimes, this correction and recalculation must be embedded into the standard 'business as usual' payroll process pending correction of the payroll application itself.

More recently, there has been a perceived need to provide a 'light-weight' remediation service for smaller payroll users. This service is under development.

3. BUSINESS CONTEXT

The Complexity

In 2003, the NZ Government passed the Holidays Act (2003), which has ultimately proven to be complex legislation that cannot be implemented in payroll systems through configuration, with the proportion of non-compliant systems estimated to be up to 80 percent.

The complexity arises because the payroll systems usually calculate payroll on an hourly basis for wage workers, or on fixed periodic payments for salaried workers. In both cases, and somewhat intuitively, holiday entitlements are usually calculated by these systems on the same basis as the regular payments.

Unfortunately, the Act requires leave payments to be calculated at a daily rate that is the higher of: the average daily rate of the last four weeks; or the average daily rate of the last 12 months.

This causes an immediate issue because daily payments are not standard calculations for payroll systems, so that there is a need to convert wage or salary payments into daily equivalents, each of which incurs different issues.

The hourly calculation must take into account not just all hours worked, but the rates paid for the hours, including overtime rates and other time-based allowances that increase the effective per hour rate. For instance, work that flows over onto a public holiday can trigger an additional payment that must be rolled back into the period to which it relates.

For the salaried workers, the daily rate varies simply because of the number of working days in the month.

In both cases, all additional payments must also then be pro-rated into the period to which they apply. For instance, a weekly shift allowance will be pro-rated across all days in that week; whereas an annual bonus must be pro-rated across all days worked in that year. The scope of additional payments includes payments made for leave taken, thus adding a regressive element to the calculation. For instance, a high bonus in a month can increase the daily rate for leave taken in the following month, which will in turn increase the daily average for that month, etc.

For the sake of clarity, all payments made to employees are covered by the Act and need to be included in the calculated daily rates.

Once all amounts have been apportioned to each day's payment, the rolling four week and 12-month averages need to be calculated, so that leave taken on any given day can be paid according to the highest of these rolling averages. This requires a rolling daily recalculation because of the regressive factor i.e. each holiday payment changes the relevant averages.

Further complexity is added because holiday pay is a common element of termination pays, and so the recalculation and remediation must include all terminated employees, with a six-year remediation horizon defined by the Act.

Notwithstanding the above already complex scenario, the largest challenge in all of the projects has been quality of data and undisciplined use of the systems.

For example:

- 'Annual Leave' payment code is sometimes used both for 'Annual Leave Taken' and 'Annual Leave Entitlement' paid out on termination of the employment. These need to be treated differently depending on where in the employment period they appear.
- It has also been seen that some organizations do not separately record 'Public Holiday Observed' with its own pay code, so in these cases a diary of all public holidays needs to be kept to generate these entries, as the Act stipulates that a 'Public Holiday Observed' needs to be paid according to a formula in the Act.
- Situations where balances and hours paid have, in accordance with ancient practices, been cleared following payment have also been encountered so that these values have had to be regenerated from first principles.

With the above as background, we can now overlay the commercial reality of a recalculation and remediation. The employer, who has paid in good faith to date, is now charged with the cost of remediation, and any additional payouts that are incurred, which can be substantial. This creates price sensitivity.

At the same time, the employees have by now discovered that they have been paid incorrectly under the Act and are concerned to verify that the remediation and go forward payments are correct.

And due to the complexity of the Act, both require a trusted third-party advisor who can authoritatively warrant that the payments are correct following remediation. Deloitte provide expert payroll consultancy services to customers throughout NZ and are perfectly suited to this role.

However, in 2014 when the first remediation was being negotiated with NZ Police, there was no technically viable solution for the automated recalculation and remediation required. At this point, Deloitte sought a rules-based solution, and the Police remediation project became the trailblazer for many subsequent remediations.

4. THE KEY INNOVATIONS

4.1 Business and Operational Impact

Why Do Customers Seek Remediation?

There are significant and compelling reasons for prompt and efficient remediation of payrolls in error.

First and foremost, following a recent adjustment to the Employment Relations Act, the Labour Inspectorate (the NZ Government Labour Regulator) is empowered to audit payrolls without cause, and substantial civil penalties can be imposed on companies that do not comply with the Act. Such penalties, if incurred, would almost certainly exceed the cost of calculating and paying remediation.

Secondly, the legal and financial perils that are implicit in any company's payroll is an issue for all stakeholders, with particular emphasis on any company involved with merger or acquisition activities. These perils must be quantified and remediated before the mergers and acquisitions can take place without legal and financial risk.

National Importance

The cost of calculating the remediation is a direct imposition on the national economy. An efficient process for this is of national importance.

Also, the employees invariably benefit from the recalculation and remediation, meaning significant wealth redistribution throughout the economy.

The Rules Topology

Using their expert understanding of the Act and of the payroll systems in the market, Deloitte was able to develop a conceptual recalculation and remediation approach to be implemented by rules.

This approach resulted in the rules topology in the diagram below.

PAYROLL REMEDIATION RULES TOPOLOGY

Diagram Narrative

In this diagram (see above), an arrow represents the flow of data as a single XML document per employee for the entire remediation period (six plus one years). All data required by the process is described in this record. The XML is read and updated by the various decision models (square boxes) as it passes through them. A decision model is a complete multi-step algorithm that achieves the purpose of the model indicated by its label and the related discussion in this document.

The top tier of the Diagram represents the various payroll systems in the market. Eight different vendor systems have been remediated to date, including global brands.

The process starts by mapping the payroll data to the XML using mapping technology provided by the rules' product vendor.

This starts an iterative process of validation and correction of the input data. As might be expected, this part of the process is the lengthiest and most arduous.

A standard model for each payroll system is used to perform the validations and correct known issues for that payroll platform. These are supplemented by customer specific models to make further adjustments to correct any issues that arise from that customer's specific use of the payroll platform, which can vary over time under different administrators.

When the data passes the validation gate and is deemed (by the rules) to be valid for the remediation process, it is processed by the transformation model(s). This model turns raw payroll data into the daily rate format that is used by the Holidays Act Model. The output of the transformation includes the average daily rates for the entire seven-years.

The Holidays Act model is a pure and concise implementation of the Act and has been warranted by Deloitte experts as an accurate implementation of the Act. It is never varied for a customer or payroll system.

The Holidays Act Model calculates the correct holiday payments for comparison with the actual payments made.

When complete, the XML flows to the reporting Model, which calculates each day's remediation adjustment, and then transforms the entire XML into a format that corresponds to an Excel spreadsheet. The final step is to convert the employee XML to Excel, which is distributed to the parties to provide the definitive audit trail and final report for the regulator, the employer, the employee, and their advisors.

Iterative Process

Building out the models has been a continuous process that 'learns' with each customer engagement. There have been more than 20 engagements to date covering hundreds of thousands of employees and generating substantial payouts. As each improvement is made, the process becomes more accurate, faster, and less resource intensive, and is now the most cost efficient and accurate solution in the market (some alternative approaches have been audited post remediation and found to still not be compliant!).

Notwithstanding an efficient process, the full process cycle described above is a substantial and expensive engagement even for Tier 1 customers.

For smaller employers, a more cost-effective solution is required. So more recently, the approach has been adjusted to allow customers to supply their own data via Excel that is manually prepared to comply with the input requirements of the Holidays Act Model, which will be made available on a SaaS basis to achieve the same end as the Tier 1 solution without a requirement for high levels of consulting. This approach is still under development.

Deloitte NZ compete in this space with their global competitors. Deloitte believe that the rules-based solution now being used is the most efficient in the market, and all else being equal, this means that they are inherently better able to compete.

A separate business unit has been established for this purpose, which is now generating significant and profitable revenues for Deloitte NZ.

4.2 Innovation

Payrolls are traditionally complex applications. This complexity arises from the variability of national legislation, the number of discrete calculations involved, and the propensity for frequent variations in contract terms and conditions across various groups of workers and across time.

By way of example, the Queensland Health Department (Australia) has now acknowledged a $AUD1.4bn blowout on a payroll implementation for an approximate workforce of 100,000. More recently, Canada has acknowledged a similar size failure across its Federal payroll systems in the Phoenix project, which has now been abandoned. And in NZ, the ~100,000 teachers payroll system for the Ministry of Education has had a $NZD100m cost blowout. The point of these examples is to emphasize that payroll is complex and non-trivial, even without the Act.

In order to assess the NZ holiday entitlement, there is a need to ensure that the proximate daily rates can be established, which means recalculating items including base pay, overtime, holidays, allowances, cash-ups, long service leave, etc. That is, the entire payroll needs to be recalculated and refactored to determine effective daily rates for every day for the full seven-years. Only then can the correct holiday pay be determined, which is a critical input into the final adjustment calculation. Note that any change in system or administrator during the seven years compounds this complexity.

In this solution, an adjustment amount per day for six years is calculated, and then mapped into an Excel spreadsheet along with supporting data for full disclosure to the employee and their advisors.

During the remediation process, Payroll systems are often found to have systemic inaccuracies, which require rules-based correction before complete recalculation of the payroll can be attempted. Sometimes, the correction and recalculation must be embedded into the standard payroll process pending correction of the payroll application itself. This is easily done by simply injecting the relevant decision model(s) into the underlying payroll system's processing cycle.

A critical innovation that was applied to this project was the development of a rules topography as described in the previous topic. A rules topography lays out a map of the rules architecture that guides the analysis and development of rules and is somewhat comparable to a data architecture. It is a critical step for the normalization of rules and helps to ensure that rules development is fully normalized.

A rules topography lays out the topics that have strong rules cohesion within them. These topics often align with areas of organizational or consulting expertise and define areas of rules reuse. In the case of this project, the rules are built in layers around the core Holidays Act model, so that only customer-specific differences need to be codified into customer specific decision models. Decision models that pre-exist for different vendors systems are reusable across customers, as are other layers of transformation and validation rules as the data migrates from the source systems through to the central Holidays Act model.

4.3 Impact and Implementation

The NZ Police Payroll Remediation

The NZ Police payroll remediation is the reference case that exemplifies the generic Deloitte solution. In 2014, the existing Police payroll system was reviewed to assess the correctness of termination pay and was found to have multiple systemic errors over a period of decades. The Regulator required a recalculation and determination of per member adjustments for all members terminated between 1/4/2004 and 27/10/2011.

Deloitte was retained to undertake the recalculation and remediation.

A rules-based calculation engine was developed to correct the payroll calculation errors and reprocess all termination payments for people terminated in the relevant period to determine their correct pay in accordance with the NZ Holidays Act 2003. Then to calculate deltas against actuals and generate remediation payments (total value approaching $NZD3m).

Following the successful conclusion of the Termination Pay Project, Deloitte was further requested by NZ Police to recalculate all payments covered by the Holidays Act 2003 (i.e. not just termination payments) and to remediate several issues under their collective agreements. This resulted in a further total remediation payout exceeding $NZD40m. Per member reconciliation spreadsheets were produced to provide full transparency of the recalculations over six years.

The general approach for recalculation and remediation of payrolls to comply with the Act was developed at this time. Using the Police project as a reference case, the project was required to:

- Retrieve the required source data from the Payroll System Database (e.g. Employment Details, Allowances, Payments Made, Leave Taken, LWOP Days etc.)
- Construct an intermediate data structure suitable for the analysis
- Calculate what the payments should have been and compared these with payments made
- Produce a report with references to the individual inputs and the intermediate calculated structures to provide a detailed audit trail to support remediation payments (or the lack thereof).

The complexities involved in this project included:

- The underlying payroll systems have varying data quality, including inconsistent and irregular data (e.g. leave taken following termination)
- Data structures and database keys changing over time as systems migrated
- Running different Calendars for different parts of the country
- Data to be analyzed reached as far back as 8 years
- All nuances in the Holidays Act over the full-term including definitions of Base Rate, Ordinary Rate and Average Weekly Earnings
- Creating an intermediate data structure representing each day the person was employed, to be marked with the amount the employee was paid that day in aggregate, or if leave was taken
- Calculating TOIL and Special Care Cash Ups
- Calculating Annual Leave, Long Service Leave, Shift Workers Leave and Statutory Holiday pay outs
- Comparing the Calculated Amount to the Amount Paid
- The Amount Paid was not uniformly found and needed to be located from different places depending on time period
- Refactoring the results into a day-by-day report format to be published as Excel for the employee and their advisors.

Following the remediation described above, it became apparent that payroll systems throughout NZ were not calculating correctly according to the Holidays Act. In April 2016, the Government increased employer obligations to correct this, and penalties for failure accordingly. The Labour regulator was further empowered and has issued a number of actionable enforcements.

At this time, Deloitte formed a Centre of Excellence (2-3 people) with support from the rules' product vendor, and the solution that is described herein was productized and taken to market. The COE is responsible for the continued evolution of the reusable models throughout the solution, and for training new consultants on a regular basis as the team expands.

5. HURDLES OVERCOME

5.1 Management

Building an efficient process for the full cycle from customer engagement through to final remediation and payout required building a multi-disciplinary team in a new business unit.

The team's resources include the following skillsets: sales, customer account management, payroll subject matter experts, payroll vendor system experts, database experts, rules authors, and testers. The team is split across two organisations

This unit was modelled on a military style task-force, where all required skills belong to a common reporting structure, and prior organisation or role boundaries cease to be relevant when the team is operational.

5.2 Business

The new business unit has had to meet the needs of managing up to ten customers at a time in the presales process, and then pipelining up to eight remediation projects in parallel on a continuous basis through the team's processes.

The task-force approach has proven effective in meeting this need with a minimum of resources.

Notwithstanding the efficiency of the process when compared with competitors, the entire topic is a substantial net cost to the employers, and there is significant price resistance. As a result, short form remediations are being developed, where employers can simply supply pre-defined datasets (database, XML, or Excel/CSV) for interpretation by the Holidays Act model. A Software-as-a-Service approach is being investigated.

5.3 Organization Adoption

This is a new and self-contained business unit established by Deloitte for this purpose.

Nonetheless, there are now multiple other use cases for the underlying rules capability that are being investigated by Deloitte across multiple jurisdictions.

6. BENEFITS

6.1 Cost Savings / Time Reductions

This process is simply the most efficient in the market when measured by hours to achieve the outcome and provides a substantial hurdle for competitors. The more recent short form and SaaS process options will expand the market to include smaller employers and reduce costs further for employers that take advantage of it.

6.2 Increased Revenues

This process has built a profitable new revenue stream from a dedicated unit.

The process has built core IP in the form of the Holidays Act model and various transformation models for different vendor Payroll systems. This IP is owned by the proprietors of the business unit and is separately charged as an add-on to the consulting fees. This improves top-line and bottom-line revenue when compared with the standard consulting revenue model.

6.3 Quality Improvements

This process has codified best practice and provides verifiable assurance of compliance. This is reassuring for the employer and the employees.

Depending on the depth of the investigation employed, there is often a side effect of general payroll verification and/or identification of anomalies that require correction in the underlying system.

7. BEST PRACTICES, LEARNING POINTS AND PITFALLS

7.1 Best Practices and Learning Points

✓ Developing a rules topography to guide rules development is an important precursor step to take in any rules development and is essential for effective normalization of rules.

✓ Rules should be fully normalized – this means the fewest number of rules to implement the required algorithms, which by definition means that the algorithm is in its simplest form.

✓ Normalized rules allow greater agility (less to change), fewer errors, more re-use, and less development effort.

✓ When rules are normalized, it follows that patterns for reuse of rules must be achieved at many levels, with special emphasis on the decision model itself. This is the driver for a rules topology.

✓ Identify and develop the core rules first. These are the rules that define the **purpose of the system**. Then follow through with development of transformation rules, validation rules, and finally workflow and reporting rules. That is, build from the inside out, starting with the core, and working back to the inputs (via transformations and validations), and then working forward to the outputs (new state values, reports, workflows).

✓ Use the best subject matter experts to develop the reusable rules in order to codify and then leverage their expertise.

7.2 Pitfalls

✗ In general, avoid the antithesis of the above.

✗ Don't build monolithic rules structures that mix purpose and expertise.

✗ Don't mix rules by type in the same algorithm (e.g. core calculation, transformation, validation, workflow, etc.).

8. COMPETITIVE ADVANTAGES

Competitive advantage accrues from three critical areas.

Firstly, the Holidays Act itself has been codified and reviewed for accuracy. It now exists as a single decision model that is a definitive and executable version of the Act that is reusable for all payrolls.

Secondly, the speed and development efficiency of the rules tool means that existing payroll systems can be quickly re-factored from wage/salary centric to day-rate centric as required by the Holidays Act decision model.

Finally, individual contract-based calculations within any Payroll System can be quickly reconfigured as decision models to validate and/or correct systemic errors in the underlying system(s).

Considered together, these advantages ensure that no competitor can offer a faster or more accurate recalculation and remediation.

Notwithstanding, there is a concerted effort being made to continue to improve (i.e. reduce) the recalculation and remediation time and costs, particularly for the benefit of smaller businesses.

These efforts are focusing on building more generic transformation capabilities to feed into the proven recalculation model. Excel spreadsheets are a viable medium for supply of payroll data for smaller employers because these can be more easily developed and populated by businesses without in-house IT shops.

When the Excel input schema and process model is available, it is likely to be provided under a SaaS model for unattended use by the employer/customer. Access to an individual verification model for use by individual employees is also under consideration, also to be made available under a fee-based SaaS model.

9. TECHNOLOGY

The technology used for rules offers many compelling features:

Scale and Complexity of Rules: The rules development paradigm, and its supporting decision engine, is required to deal with all terms and conditions found in employment contracts across the full extent of the labor market, as well as all standard payroll calculations, and the calculations required by the Act.

The recalculation process uses a variety of decisioning techniques such as: derivation, augmentation, aggregation, creation, generation, accumulation, date boundary, and general pattern matching to assemble and convert the raw payroll data into a format that can be used for recalculation and remediation for compliance with the Act.

We process seven-years of complete payroll data per employee in a single XML record, with the largest employer in NZ having circa 100,000 employees. Note that seven-years is likely to span many sets of employment terms and conditions, and occasionally spans payroll systems boundaries when the payroll customer switches systems. We have also found that changes in administrative behavior throughout the 7year term mean that the use and meaning of different data elements varies over time. These changes in use and meaning are material but not obvious; when found, additional rules are generally required to standardize the data in these fields.

Performance: While calculations are not required in real time, it is important that elapsed run-time is acceptable (a few hours max) to effectively support the development and testing process. It is a feature of the rules' technology used that the rules engine is both stateless and thread-safe. The rules development paradigm explicitly focuses on entity level data and calculation, in this case, an individual employee. Every available thread can be used to process an employee entity end-to-end.

The vendor-supplied Mapping technology supports multiple processes, each of which runs multiple threads. In general, one core can run slightly more than one process. Therefore, the number of cores and processes required for adequate run-times is determined by the size of the payroll file, in particular the number of employees. Our largest payroll to date has used 32 cores to run 40 processes in parallel, usually processing a member end-to-end in about one second. The more complex Police project final production run was completed in four hours, using data extracted from an Oracle Database and processed by six parallel run-time processes (around two seconds per employee).

Ease of Use: The above techniques must be easily accessible to Deloitte's payroll subject matter experts [SME] using graphical, language neutral interfaces.

The rules development is performed by the team of Deloitte consultants. Training in the tool and the substantial range of pre-existing models is required regularly. This training is provided by the 'center of excellence', which is also continuing to evolve the pre-existing models as new edge cases come to hand. Training takes 1-3 days, depending on the complexity of the immediate target payrolls.

Data Agility: A simple change to an XML schema is all that is required to introduce new facts into the scope of the rules. Data can be added at will on an ongoing basis and are immediately available to subsequent rules processing.

This data is supplied to the rules by the vendor supplied mapping tool that explicitly supports the decision engine processing cycle. The mapping tool reads the source data and assembles it into entity level XML (one per employee) very quickly; it then distributes it across as many rules engine instances as required to achieve the desired throughput.

Time Sensitive: The rules tool uses effective dates at all levels, across all components, from individual data items, through individual logical operations, formulas, and any aggregation of the same through to entire decision models. This effective dating means that one decision model can easily manage contract terms and conditions that change on annual boundaries and is critical if there has been a system change within the 7-year period, which generally requires a substantial change in the processing model at an arbitrary date.

On Board Execution: The rules tool has an on-board execution engine and extensive support for both on-board step-by-step and full regression/simulation testing. This allows an independent rules development cycle that means rules can be developed independently of the application(s) they will service.

For payroll remediation, rules must be able to be developed and tested in isolation, using masked data use-cases. There are multiple reasons for this. Firstly, privacy issues limit the movement and distribution of live data. Secondly, the Payroll customer is not always in a position to provide the required processing capacity and access to the full payroll in a timely manner for the remediation team, while continuous on-site development (even via VPN, which is not always available) is awkward and time consuming. Self-provisioning is important.

Accordingly, the on-board execution capability is fully utilized for development and unit testing, with payroll runs on live data only used for UAT and production runs.

10. THE TECHNOLOGY AND SERVICE PROVIDERS

Deloitte Limited https://www2.deloitte.com/nz/en.html

Deloitte brings together more than 1,200 specialists providing New Zealand's widest range of high-quality professional services. We focus on audit, tax, technology & systems, strategy, performance improvements, risk management, corporate finance, business recovery, forensics and accounting services.

IDIOM Limited www.idiomsoftware.com

IDIOM supplies the IDIOM Decision Manager™, which was used to construct all decision models referenced in this case study. IDIOM Decision Manager™ is a graphical modelling tool that is used by subject matter experts to build, test, and deploy very large and complex decision models for any domain.

IDIOM also supplies the IDIOM Mapper™, which is used to acquire data from a relational database or other sources, to render it for use by decision models, and to then execute the decision models at scale.

IBM Global Sales Incentives
IBM Corporation, US

1. EXECUTIVE SUMMARY / ABSTRACT

Using Robotics Process Automation (RPA) software, IBM has created an automated process to have a robot work as a delegate for sales managers. This robot, named Nano Second, can create Incentive Plan Letters (IPL) for sellers on a specific type of sales incentive plan known as a Pool Plan. The IPL is the formal agreement between IBM and each person who is eligible to be on an incentive plan. Having invented a robot to follow a specific set of business rules and create the IPLs for 2H 2017 Pool Plans, has freed sales managers from manually entering data from other systems into the system where the IPLs are created and tracked. This has provided them with more time for other more productive engagements with their sellers and clients.

In the past, managers would typically spend about 10 minutes per IPL creation. With the creation of Nano, IPLs for thousands of sellers worldwide, are created in an average of 18 seconds per letter. In total, during each cycle, sales managers who have benefited from this new process, have saved on average, about 70 minutes each.

2. OVERVIEW

IBM is moving to Robotics Process Automation (RPA) in order to reduce manual tasks in processes, help things move faster, reduce errors, and deliver results by eliminating administrative or repetitive tasks. Using RPA frees employees up and enables them to focus on higher value work. IBM's Global Sales Incentives (GSI) organization has embraced RPA to lessen workloads of sales managers and sales incentives support personnel, freeing them up to spend more time engaging with their sellers and clients.

The concept of RPA is very similar to a flowcharter in a virtual environment. The software robot can be configured using rules-based logic to perform tasks such as cutting and pasting data from a spreadsheet into an application, in order to perform a particular task. The robot uses keyboard and mouse controls to take actions and execute automations. Business operations employees - people with process and subject matter expertise but no programing experience - can be trained to independently automate processes using RPA tools within a few weeks. The robot accesses end user computer systems - via the user interface with an established access control mechanism (e.g. logon ID and password) - so no underlying systems programming is required.

The first implementation was focused on the Incentive Plan Letter (IPL) for sellers on a particular type of incentive plan known as a Pool Plan. The IPL is the formal agreement between an eligible employee and IBM. This agreement allows eligible employees to be compensated for the sale of products and services directly to a specific set of customers, business partners and/or territories responsible for driving incremental revenue, profit and/or signings. The sales managers are ultimately responsible for creating, updating, and cancelling IPLs.

The Pool Plan sellers for 2H 2017 were identified by specific sales roles by having the robot run a query in the incentives database and extracting the data into a spreadsheet. The robot then logged in as a delegate for the sales managers in IBM's legacy system tool. This RPA process involved input into multiple screens following IBM's business rules for the creation of Incentive Plan Letters. The robot then notified the sales managers about the draft IPLs that were created. The sales managers reviewed the draft IPLs and then offered them to the sellers for final acceptance.

3. BUSINESS CONTEXT

Prior to the use of the RPA process for IPL creation, managers had to manually compile information about their sellers such as job role, plan type and incentive element details. They would then need to log into IBM's legacy system tool and manually input data on multiple screens in order to create the IPLs for offering to their respective sellers.

With the creation of Nano, IPLs for thousands of sellers worldwide, are created in an average of 18 seconds per letter, saving sales managers on average, about 70 minutes each.

4. THE KEY INNOVATIONS

4.1 Business and Operational Impact
- Worldwide creation of more than 7,000 Incentive Plan Letters (IPLs)
- IPL creation improved from 10 minutes to 18 seconds per letter
- Average time savings of 70 minutes per sales manager
- Managers freed up to focus on higher value activities
  - Sales activities
  - Client engagements
  - Employee coaching/mentoring
- Accelerated 2H 2017 Start-up of new sales cycle
  - Incentive Plan Letters were able to be issued in a timely manner.
  - Met target of 98% of sellers on Plan 30 days sooner compared to prior year.
- Better data quality with automated inputs vs. manual inputs
- Much more cost-effective solution compared to development of a more expensive replacement of legacy systems.

4.2 Innovation
- Integration of RPA with existing tools and processes drives efficiency and productivity through automation.
- Using internal organization resources with business owner subject matter experts to develop and deploy RPA solutions is more effective and accelerated approach as compared to costly IT investments in reprogramming legacy systems.
- RPA can be used to access all kinds of applications from modern web solutions to legacy mainframe software which allows for flexibility to implement solutions to existing business rules across the organization.
- Changes in business processes can be easily updated using the RPA processes and tools.

4.3 Impact and Implementation
- The successful implementation of the Pool Plan IPL creation using robotics was met with great appreciation by the sales managers evidenced by this sampling of feedback:
  - "I must say, a great process improvement."
  - "Great progress for IPL deployment."

- o "Just to let you know that the enhancement made with pre/filled in information really has been helpful and speeded up the process."
- The RPA solution is easily scalable to all worldwide sale plan types (Individual Quota, Absolute and Pool Plans), evidenced by the creation of over 20,000 IPLs for 1H 2018 and the expectation of nearly 30,000 IPLs to be created for the 2H 2018 sales cycle.
- The organization is now identifying other business processes which involve manual and repetitive steps as candidates for future RPA solutions like:
  - o Generation of specific and targeted automation e-mails
  - o Query/Report processing
  - o Automated refreshes of cognitive dashboards and presentations

5. HURDLES OVERCOME

5.1 Management
- The management challenge was to ensure that controls were in place to mitigate any business controls exposure
  - o Robot was set with unique userid credentials.
  - o All transactions processed by the robot were identifiable and trackable.

- **Business**
- The business challenge was to gain knowledge and build RPA skills with existing organizational resources
  - o RPA workshops and boot camps assisted with training and development.
  - o Acquisition of laptops with faster processors to handle speed/volumes.

- **Organization Adoption**
  - o RPA solutions have freed up time spent on manual and repetitive tasks, redirecting the focus on higher value tasks (i.e. Customer engagements, deeper analysis, coaching/mentoring, acquiring/building skills).
  - o Teams learned new skills at all stages of deployment.
  - o Robotics has been made fun in the organization by "humanizing" the robot by giving it a name and face – Nano Second.

6. BENEFITS

6.1 Cost Savings / Time Reductions
- IPL creation improved from an average of 10 minutes to 18 seconds per letter.
- Average time savings of 70 minutes per sales manager.

- Met target of 98% of sellers on Plan 30 days sooner compared to prior year.

6.2 Increased Revenues

- When sellers and sales managers have more time to spend with clients and teams it supports revenue growth.

6.3 Quality Improvements

- Reducing keystrokes from trusted source data with automated input increases document accuracy and timeliness.

7. BEST PRACTICES, LEARNING POINTS AND PITFALLS

7.1 Best Practices and Learning Points

- *Ensure Subject Matter Experts are engaged in development of the RPA solutions*
- *RPA solutions are scalable and easily adaptable to other business processes using existing tools*
- *"Humanize" the robot to portray as a team member (i.e. name, picture, doll, etc.)*
- *Engage multiple worldwide resources across the organization for automation ideas to help build a backlog and gain buy-in from the teams*
- *Remove process inefficiencies to maximize automation*
- *Use video recording options to assist with process flow/requirements*
- *Celebrate successes*

7.2 Pitfalls

- *Start small and then scale*
- *Don't have too many projects to deliver on at the same time*
- *Don't automate from management directives, but rather from bottoms up*

8. COMPETITIVE ADVANTAGES

- There is tremendous upside in cost efficiency, savings, and productivity among other global organizations, both for our commissions support personnel and our salespeople. As noted in Section 4, our robot Nano Second can scale to heightened levels of workload volume (tens of thousands of Incentive Plan Letters across the globe) based on complex business rules. This generates significant impact on business operations and seller satisfaction.
- With an Incentive Plan Letter in place sooner than was historically done, the seller is more focused and motivated early on in the sales cycle, regarding what to sell based on their plan, with a clear line of sight as to how they will be compensated. This not only improves seller satisfaction, but ultimately drive revenue as well.
- The Nano Second project tightly aligns to our business strategy around workforce and cognition vis-à-vis robotic processing—specifically, transforming our employees to higher-skilled roles where they allow technology to execute processing while focusing their attention on review, analysis, and decision making. This is about shifting the repetitive, rules-driven work onto our Nano Second robot with controls in place to ensure quality with less manual effort. IBM is very proud of creating and applying innovation like this to drive efficiency and productivity on such a huge scale.

9. TECHNOLOGY

- Simple automation using presentation integration (RPA software) can eliminate errors, reduce costs and perform high volume transactional work in a fraction of the time it takes humans.
- RPA software can be used to access all kinds of applications, from modern Web solutions to legacy mainframe software.
- A digital workforce is ideally suited to handle tasks that either happen too fast for humans to respond or too often to be worth human time to complete.
- The impetus is not necessarily to replace people, but to transform the work that humans do and create new ways of working.
- The human workforce recaptures time to do what it's best suited to do: think strategically, act creatively and interact humanely.

10. THE TECHNOLOGY AND SERVICE PROVIDERS

http://www.blueprism.com/

IISSB at Centers for Disease Control and Prevention (CDC), USA

Nominated by CDC/IISSB, USA

Warren Williams, David Lyalin, Stuart Myerburg, Eric Larson, Loren Rodgers, Lauren Shaw, Kristen Seer

1. EXECUTIVE SUMMARY / ABSTRACT

The Immunization Information Systems Support Branch (IISSB) at the Centers for Disease Control and Prevention (CDC) "works to maximize protection against vaccine-preventable diseases by leading the advancement of immunization information systems (IIS)".[i]

Several years ago, IISSB embarked on a journey to implement a business rules approach to address issues with communication and interpretation of common immunization rules and IIS best practices. This journey evolved from the introduction of new business analysis techniques and a new rule management tool to the expansion of the approach to other areas within IISSB.

The Modeling Immunization Registry Workgroup (MIROW), a joint initiative of IISSB and its partner, American Immunization Registry Association (AIRA)[ii], was the first to adopt these analysis techniques, using them to facilitate capturing the principles and business rules for operational best practice guides. The MIROW group is currently leveraging the rule management tool to identify areas of inconsistency and develop a common vocabulary across MIROW guides.

The next area addressed was Clinical Decision Support for Immunization (CDSi). This involved understanding the terminology used by the Advisory Committee on Immunization Practices (ACIP), interpreting the ACIP recommendations, and expressing them in the form of business rules and decision tables. The result was a well-defined CDSi Logic Specification that provides the immunization information systems community with a common solution for vaccine evaluation and forecasting.

Most recently, the IIS Functional Standards and the logic for measuring progress towards meeting the standards (based on IIS Annual Report (IISAR) data) have been captured in the rule management tool to facilitate management of the relationships between the standards, operational guidance statements, and the progress towards goals.

The benefits of implementing a business rules approach and rule management tool have included:

- Better communication amongst stakeholders
- Business rules that are comprehensible by public health professionals yet rigorous enough for implementers
- Improved reusability, consistency and accuracy of business rules
- Decision logic understood and validated by both business and developers prior to system design
- Comprehensive impact analysis for changes to business rules.

2. OVERVIEW

The Immunization Information Systems Support Branch (IISSB) at the Centers for Disease Control and Prevention (CDC) "works to maximize protection against vaccine-preventable diseases by leading the advancement of immunization information systems (IIS). Immunization information systems help to maximize protection against vaccine-preventable diseases by providing accurate data on which to make informed immunization decisions".[iii]

The IISSB provides guidance and information to the IIS community in the form of IIS functional standards, guidelines, specifications, and recommendations.

The IIS community implements the best practices, policies and business rules for immunization. The IIS community includes:

- Various agencies at the state, county, and municipal levels
- Software vendors, including vendors of Clinical Decision Support (CDS) engines
- Public Health Consultants.

Several years ago, the IISSB embarked on a journey to implement a business rules approach to address issues with development, communication and interpretation of clinical guidance and IIS best practices. This journey evolved from the introduction of new analysis techniques and selection of a rule management tool to the expansion of the approach to other areas within IISSB.

There are three main tracks where the business rules approach has been applied:

- Modeling Immunization Registry Workgroup (MIROW)
- Clinical Decision Support for Immunization (CDSi)
- IIS Functional Standards and measures.

Track 1: MIROW

The Modeling Immunization Registry Workgroup (MIROW), a committee of IISSB's partner, American Immunization Registry Association (AIRA)[iv], was the first area where IISSB applied business analysis techniques, using them to facilitate capturing the principles and business rules for operational best practice guides aimed at the IIS community. The best practice guides cover complex topics such as:

- Managing vaccine inventory
- Consolidating demographic and vaccination event records
- Vaccination level deduplication.

IISSB's goal was to:

- Improve collaboration and communication amongst the diverse stakeholders brought together to create each guide
- Ensure each guide communicated the best practices in a user-friendly manner and as clearly and concisely as possible.

Some of the challenges included:

- With different stakeholders and topics for each guide, it was difficult to leverage the work of previous efforts as there was no common terminology or approach to capturing the business rules.
- The analysis techniques were new to most of the stakeholders and required an initial adjustment before the team could start working effectively.
- The wording of the rules needed to be flexible because the guides offer guidelines on best practices rather than strict standards.

The rule management tool was used to harvest the terms, principles and business rules after-the-fact to identify areas of inconsistency in terminology and anomalies in the rules.

The MIROW group has recently started to leverage the tool to identify areas of inconsistency in the terminology in order to move towards a single concept model shared across the best practice guides.

Track 2: CDSi

The next area we addressed was Clinical Decision Support for Immunization (CDSi). This involved understanding the terminology used by the Advisory Committee on Immunization Practices (ACIP), interpreting the ACIP recommendations for immunization, and expressing them in the form of business rules and decision tables. These components were published in a document called the "CDSi Logic Specification" which is used by the IIS community as input to the analysis and design process for their immunization information systems. This helps to ensure that the ACIP recommendations are implemented consistently in the various state, county and municipal-level IIS.

The rule management tool is used to maintain the terms, rules and decision tables, then output them to the CDSi Logic Specification. The CDSi Logic Specification is published as a free resource by the IISSB.

Some of the challenges we encountered were in interpreting the science-based prose in the ACIP recommendations into a more structured form, particularly regarding the timing of the immunizations (e.g., administering a vaccine at a certain age or at a certain interval from the last vaccination). The rules and decision tables needed to be expressed rigorously to minimize misinterpretation by a largely non-medical audience.

The result of this initiative is a well-defined, easily-maintained CDSi Logic Specification that provides the IIS community with a common solution for implementation in their CDS Engine. This in turn has resulted in an increase in the accuracy and consistency of immunization evaluation and forecasting.

Track 3: IIS Functional Standards & Measures

IISSB is also responsible for establishing the IIS Functional Standards that "describe the operations, data quality, and technology needed by IISs to support immunization programs, vaccination providers, and other immunization stakeholders and their immunization-related goals".[v]

IISSB provides a self-administered web-based questionnaire called the IIS Annual Report (IISAR) to help the IIS community assess their progress towards meeting the standards.

The IIS Functional Standards and the measures from the IISAR are captured in the rule management tool to facilitate management of the relationships between the standards and the progress towards goals. The measures, which are primarily in the form of computations, are organized by the IIS Functional Standards.

The challenges involved how to name and structure the computational rules to be as plain language as possible while still being rigorous enough for implementation in various statistical and reporting tools.

The result of this initiative is a greater ability to do impact analysis of changes to the rules as each new IIS Annual Report is developed.

3. BUSINESS CONTEXT

In the United States, there is no central IIS. Each jurisdiction (states, a few cities, and territories) operates their own IIS. Because of differences in resources (both personnel and technical), there was a wide variety of practices and data quality in these systems prior to initiatives to improve standardization. The CDC/IISSB had multiple efforts ongoing to support jurisdictions with their systems. Given the federated nature of the public health enterprise, any attempts at community-wide guidance would need to be developed through the collaboration and consensus of the IIS community. Prior to these and other similar efforts, technical assistance was provided to jurisdictions on an individual basis. Because each system was unique, assistance from the CDC had to be unique to the jurisdiction as well.

4. THE KEY INNOVATIONS

The following impacts resulted from the three tracks:

4.1 Business and Operational Impact

MIROW

- IISSB is able to provide valuable resources on best practices to the IIS community to improve the alignment and uniformity of immunization information systems.
- The MIROW operational best practice guides follow a consistent approach, improving comprehension and increasing the chances of adoption by the IIS community.
- Consensus amongst the disparate stakeholders is more quickly achieved through using a structured, business-oriented approach.
- IISSB is able to provide traceability for each term and rule to the operational best practice guide(s) where it used.

CDSi

- IISSB is able to provide valuable resources to the IIS community to improve consistency and quality of immunization evaluation and forecasting.
- The IIS community can save significant development time for their IIS by leveraging the analysis done in the CDSi Logic Specification.
- Changes to the ACIP recommendations are quickly reflected in the CDSi Logic Specification, enabling the IIS community to more quickly implement the changes in their IIS.
- IISSB is able to provide traceability from the ACIP recommendations to the business rules and decision tables interpreted from those recommendations.
- IISSB is able to provide traceability of the changes in the CDSi Logic Specification through its various versions.
- The IIS community is better able to demonstrate compliance with the ACIP recommendations through use of the CDSi Logic Specification.
- Immunization evaluation and forecasting have more consistent outcomes, thereby improving the immunization decisions made by health care providers.

IIS Functional Standards & Measures

- The computations are more precisely specified using the rules, thereby improving the accuracy of the outcomes.

- The terms and rules are traced from their sources to their implementation, clearly laying out how to go from one product (e.g. IIS Annual Report) to another (e.g., various statistical reports).
- Anomalies in the calculations are more easily identified.

4.2 Innovation

- ACIP recommendations can be complex. This approach reduced the prose description by ACIP into logic that could be used by different audiences. This included determining the best format to express rules.
- A solution that could be used by multiple audiences for vaccine evaluation and forecasting was created.
- A method for supporting the changing and complex business process of translating the IISAR to a user-friendly dashboard was established.
- The approaches provided consistency in terminology across products, leading to standardization. Instead of operating in individual silos, each sector had more collaboration and a greater level of integration.
- Business agility to adapt to changing recommendations improved with this approach.
- These approaches have not been previously used in this area of public health or in the well-established field of clinical decision support. They provided a unique solution.
  For MIROW, concept modelling using the rule management tool has helped to achieve notable results in gaining consensus on the terminology.

4.3 Impact and Implementation

- The commitment of IISSB to introducing a business rules approach is significant in terms of resources. It has entailed a different way of thinking and noteworthy discipline on the part of the staff.
- The initial focus for all the tracks was on improving the analysis toolkit for the employees and contractors. This included learning:
  o Concept modeling
  o Rule expression
  o Use of decision tables
  o Organization of rules
- Most of the terms and rules were discovered and expressed outside the rule management tool and then imported after the fact into the tool as part of a concerted effort.
- The approach is slowly shifting to using the tool during the discovery and expression phases in order to leverage the rule analysis capabilities of the tool.
- The terms and rules are developed with a smaller group but are distributed to a very wide audience.
- The adoption rate of the best practice guides and the CDSi Logic Specification has been high.
- The degree of complexity of the rules is quite high. Patterns (or templates) were developed at the beginning of some of the initiatives to facilitate consistency in the expression of the rules.
- Given the constraints on resources in a governmental environment, the IISSB has been able to increase the scope of activities without increasing headcount by using a structured approach.

5. HURDLES OVERCOME

5.1 Management

The largest challenge we faced was the necessity of a paradigm shift in our sector to embrace a business rules approach. In order to have leadership support this initiative, we had to make the case that the initial investment was worth the benefits we would receive using a business rules approach. Fortunately, we had executive support for the application of modern systematic methods of analysis to public health operations and processes from the beginning.

5.2 Business

The ACIP develop recommendations on the use of vaccines in the United States. These recommendations are complicated and are presented in various formats to the public. The challenge has been turning these complex recommendations into clear and distinct business rules that systems, either IISs or electronic medical records, can use to implement their CDS Engines. We engaged the ACIP workgroups or experts to clarify their recommendations to make sure the CDSi logic specifications we published aligned with the intent of the ACIP recommendations.

5.3 Organization Adoption

Business Adoption

Due to limited resources, we are very restricted when it comes to new initiatives and customization. While we have not been able to acquire additional resources, we have worked hard to repurpose the resources we already have. We were able to train personnel on the business rules approach and explore ways for customization that did not require additional resources.

The learning curve for business analysis is quite steep. While a majority of those who work on this project are scientists, they have had little or no training in business analysis. Using a business rules approach requires a specific methodology for decision and rule management. We engaged industry experts to conduct group training and provide mentoring to learn how to adopt a business rules approach.

Our workflow is cyclical. We use the business rules approach for a portion of the work we do. We needed to find a way to make sure our work was consistent, despite being intermittent. We did this by documenting all the processes involved in a business rules approach. No matter the time that lapses between adjustments to our business rules, we can remain consistent.

6. BENEFITS

6.1 Cost Savings / Time Reductions

- Decrease in time for IIS community to implement ACIP recommendations (based on unquantified feedback from IIS community).

- For CDSi, improved turnaround time for changes due to comprehensive impact analysis.

- Collaborative development of operational consensus-based best practices is a proven strategy for creating unity, bringing people together. Collaboration of federal and state stakeholders benefits any public health program by providing common solutions instead of requiring awardees to reinvent the wheel.

- Aligning operations of state-level participants along common guidelines, which is a main goal of these efforts, is also a typical goal that many public health programs are pursuing. Hence, the approach used to develop IIS operational best practices is an example that can be followed, benefiting other public health programs, communities, and clinical organizations.

- For CDSi, surveys have provided the following feedback from the IIS community:
  - *Consistent logic that can be incorporated in our software.*
  - *The resources will become our one reference for our software logic.*
  - *We constantly review logic specs to train new developers and evaluate how we can more fully implement CDSi.*
  - *We refer to the CDSi Logic Specification when reviewing existing functionality or adding functionality to our software.*

6.2 Quality Improvements

- For CDSi, results from a survey[vi] conducted from 2016 indicated:
  - 77 percent satisfaction with the CDSi Logic Specification
  - 87 percent had a very positive or somewhat positive impact in terms of the ease of use in developing and maintaining CDS logic using the CDSi Logic Specification.
- Comments from the CDSi surveys conducted from 2015-2018 included:
  - *CDSi supporting data and logic specification have been useful tools in bringing clarity to ACIP recommendations.*
  - *Our vaccine forecasting algorithm dramatically improved once our vendor used the CDSi logic specification to develop and maintain CDS logic. The entire CDSi project has led to dramatic, positive improvement in our vendor's forecasting algorithm.*
  - *The specifications have had a significant impact on the design of the logic in our open source software.*
  - *It provides a common language for forecasting discussions.*
  - *Standardization of application of ACIP Guidelines*
  - *Identifies options for implementing a new rule base for ACIP / Adult*
  - When asked "If a potential user was hesitant about whether to use the CDSi resources or not, what would you say to them?", one response was: *Don't delay! The future is CDSi!*
- Improved outcomes for immunization:
  - Better identification of invalid vaccinations
  - Fewer unnecessary vaccinations
  - Fewer missed vaccinations
- About 80 percent of IIS use one or more MIROW guides. Best practice guides enabled advancement and widespread uniformity of IIS operations and processes.
- Better communication amongst stakeholders due to common, well-defined terminology
- Improved reusability, consistency and accuracy of business rules
- Decision logic understood and validated by both business and developers prior to system design
- Independent evaluation findings [1] indicate that application of the MIROW best practice recommendations in the IIS domain of state and local health

departments resulted in improved data quality, reduced staff time, and increased efficiencies across immunization programs. Users of the guide reported clear advantages to not "reinventing the wheel" – business rules that reflect best practices could be directly adopted or modified as needed, which resulted in reduced IIS staff time. Also, the benefits are in increased efficiencies, a more standardized level of operational quality, and improved data validity for regional and national analyses. By working together to define best practices, significant effort can be saved across the community, and greater process standardization and more consistent operational performance achieved.[vii]

7. BEST PRACTICES, LEARNING POINTS AND PITFALLS

7.1 Best Practices and Learning Points

- ✓ Use of an industry-recognized business rule methodology enabled the team to get up to speed quickly and leverage best practices
- ✓ An evolutionary approach allowed IISSB to experiment with what worked/didn't work in their environment
- ✓ Having clear objectives (e.g., improving the clarity of the best practice guides, improving the outcomes of immunization decisions) helped keep the teams focused
- ✓ Introducing a new way of thinking takes time and patience
- ✓ Consistent rule expression and use of rule patterns enabled:
  - o faster creation of business rules
  - o greater ability to identify anomalies in the rules
- ✓ Well-defined terms and use of a concept/domain model improved communication both within the team and with stakeholders
- ✓ Central repository of knowledge enabled greater reuse of terms and rules
- ✓ Experience was gained in the methodology before selecting a rule management tool, thereby enabling a better understanding of the requirements for a repository
- ✓ Having a concept model reduces the learning curve, particularly for such a complex area (i.e., immunization)
- ✓ It's important to manage the scope. Starting with a smaller set of rules and then expanding over time helped to keep the team from being overwhelmed. For example, CDSi initially tackled only the immunization rules for children, excluding those for adults. MIROW initially dealt with one best practice guide at a time before starting to analyze the terminology shared across the guides.
- ✓ For each initiative, considerable thought was given to prior to implementation of the rule management tool in terms of:
  - o What information (meta-data) should be captured in the tool (including custom properties)
  - o How the rules should be organized
  - o What rule patterns could be leveraged (including different formats for decision tables)
  - o How to handle versioning
  - o How to manage the life cycle of the terms and rules
  - o What reporting was required
- ✓ Recommended best practices were more readily embraced because stakeholders were involved in the process and developed ownership of the resulting product.

7.2 Pitfalls

- ✗ *Trying to "boil the ocean" – that is, take on too much at a time. For example, it wasn't possible initially to get consensus on the terminology across all the best practice guides, so the focus was on getting it consistent within a single guide at a time. Now that there is greater understanding of the benefits, an effort is underway to consolidate the terminology and make it consistent throughout IISSB.*
- ✗ *Thinking about software implementation first before business analysis*
- ✗ *Thinking about rule management tools before methodology ("garbage in, garbage out")*
- ✗ *Failing to include all the stakeholders*
- ✗ *Underestimating the discipline required to ensure the consistency and quality of the concept model and business rules*
- ✗ *Not thinking about how to organize the rules beforehand*
- ✗ *Forgetting to constantly explain the rationale for using the business rules approach. People need to hear the message constantly for it to stick.*

8. COMPETITIVE ADVANTAGES

As a government agency, the CDC focuses on improving public health. The use of a business rules approach has enabled it to further its mandate by providing clear, comprehensive guidance in field of immunization.

9. TECHNOLOGY

The business rules approach used by the IISSB consisted of both a methodology and a rule management tool. These two components complemented each other, with the former providing the structure and the latter enabling more advanced capabilities.

We implemented an industry-recognized methodology covering:
- Concept modeling
- Defining terms
- Rule expression
- Decision table expression
- Rule organization
- Decision modeling

After an extensive evaluation of the marketplace, we selected a rule management tool (i.e., a business-oriented centralized repository, not a rule execution system) that enabled:
- Full analysis of the business rules
- Relationships between rules
- Versioning/history of terms and rules
- Concept modeling
- Decision analysis
- Quality analysis and reporting
- Ability to segregate communities of practices (e.g., CDSi, MIROW and IISAR)

10. THE TECHNOLOGY AND SERVICE PROVIDERS

We engaged industry leading-experts from Business Rule Solutions (BRS) (http://www.brsolutions.com). Under the direction of Gladys S.W. Lam and Ronald R. Ross, BRS provided guidance, training, and support for developing these approaches. BRS continues to provide support for maintaining these processes.

Methodologies that we employed included RuleSpeak®, DecisionSpeak™, and TableSpeak™.

The rule management tool we use is RuleXpress by RuleArts. We engaged RuleArts to generate custom reports for CDSi Logic Specification.

11. ACKNOWLEDGEMENTS

This submission was co-authored by Lauren Shaw and Kristen Seer with input from Warren Williams, David Lyalin, Stuart Myerburg, Eric Larson, and Loren Rodgers.

Introducing both the business rules approach and a business rule management tool involved the participation of numerous stakeholders both within and outside the CDC. Special thanks go to:

- Craig Newman
- Patricia Speights
- Lauren Shrader
- MIROW Co-Chairs: Elaine Lowery (AIRA Consultant) and Amanda Harris (Nevada IIS)
- MIROW Steering Committee
- MIROW Subject Matter Experts Panels

---

[i] Excerpted from the CDC website at https://www.cdc.gov/ncird/isd.html. For more information on IIS, please refer to: https://www.cdc.gov/vaccines/programs/iis/index.html

[ii] For more information on AIRA and MIROW, please refer to:

- https://www.immregistries.org
- https://www.immregistries.org/index.php?option=com_content&view=article&id=76:MIROW&catid=20:site-content&Itemid=189
- https://www.cdc.gov/vaccines/programs/iis/activities/mirow.html

[iii] Ibid. 1

[iv] Ibid. 2

[v] Excerpted from CDC website at https://www.cdc.gov/vaccines/programs/iis/func-stds.html

[vi] A new survey is currently underway to try to measure improvements in immunization outcomes; however, most of the IIS community does not have measurement systems in place, so the responses tend to be anecdotal. The results of the survey will be available in a few months and could potentially be added to this submission (pending the CDC's permission).

[vii] Dombkowski K, Cowan A, Clark S. Immunization Registry Operational Guidelines Evaluation. Final Report. University of Michigan, July 2014. Available from: http://repository.immregistries.org/resource/mirow-evaluation-final-report-and-presentation/

KPN, The Netherlands
AuraPortal, Spain

1. EXECUTIVE SUMMARY / ABSTRACT

KPN is the largest Dutch telecom and network provider with over 7.8 million mobile subscribers in the Netherlands and provides broadband access to 4.1 million customers offering business services and data transport network throughout Western Europe. KPN offers their customers the most extensive (IP) network in the Netherlands providing optimal coverage.

KPN Network Provider faced a strong growth of business and network-capacity services and an accompanying increase of operational costs. KPN Network Provider decided to transform their existing and complex fulfilment IT to support the rapidly changing market.

They defined goals based on four key aspects:

- o The customer; reduce delivery times;
- o The business; lower costs, activate real-time ethernet and IP connectivity, standardize services and gain real-time monitoring;
- o Operations; replace complex manual tasks with business rules, achieve process control and monitoring;
- o IT; reduce risk by implementing a scalable orchestrator to control processes and applications.

The project to automate technical orchestration was completed in just 18 months and consisted of three phases:

- o In the first phase, integration was developed with Network Management Systems;
- o The second phase involved implementing business rules to eliminate repetitive activities and human intelligence;
- o The final phase was linking zero-touch processes to the Service Providers, using BPM software, high-end integration, business rules and decision management.

As a result of implementing over 3,000 business rules combined with Business Process Management, First Time Right rose from <70 percent to >95 percent, delivery time from Core Roll-Out Delivery to business was reduced from five days to ten minutes and process automation increased from 21 percent to 98 percent.

2. OVERVIEW

KPN is, as a former state-owned monopolist, a Dutch telecom company that contains multiple operational telecom areas. KPN serves as a Service Provider directly to the consumer and business market through its divisions KPN Consumer Market (KPN-CM) and KPN Corporate Market (KPN-ZM).

KPN also includes a nationwide network - KPN Network Provider. This division is responsible for creating and maintaining all services, requested by internal customers (KPN-ZM and KPN-CM) and external customers, such as T-Mobile and Vodafone service providers (via KPN Wholesale).

Driven by organizational goals, such as simplifying KPN network and reducing internal costs, the project initiator was Core Roll-Out Delivery, a department of Access Core Network within the division KPN Network Provider. Their main driver was to increase efficiency within the network provider, which was necessary due to the growing workload. Besides efficiency, some of the biggest benefits have been experienced by the service providers, thanks to the elimination of production time for services and significant improvements to First Time Right (FTR) within fulfilment of Customer Services.

Implementation was a complex task, due to the challenge that production should be continued, and the customers should not notice the changes being made to the network. However, thanks to a very capable and coordinated multidisciplinary team (IT, KPN Network Provider, Core Roll-Out Delivery, internal customers and a variety of external collaborators) and agile methodology, reengineered processes with advanced business rules were successfully digitalized.

Due to agile methodology, the project team delivered value to their stakeholders every four weeks. Within one month, the first Return on Value (RoV) was created for Core Roll-Out Delivery, which made it easier to apply for subsequent budget for each phase.

Over 3,000 business rules were implemented to automate process decisioning, to make event-based decisions, for validation and to manage authorizations.

Overall, the achieved results are remarkable, positively impacting fulfilment efficiency for Core Roll-Out Delivery (reduced workload and achieved process control and monitoring) and other areas, such as IT (simplifying IT-landscape and reducing risk by implementing a scalable orchestrator to control processes and applications), internal customers (higher FTR, standardized services and real-time monitoring).

KPN considered this project as a core strategic initiative with tangible and short-term results. Furthermore, it has led the organization to a philosophy of continuous process improvement.

3. BUSINESS CONTEXT

KPN Network Provider is facing a strong growth of business and network-capacity services and an accompanying increase of operational costs. They decided to transform their existing and complex fulfilment IT to support the rapidly changing market.

Within KPN Network Provider, Core Roll-Out Delivery (project initiator) has two main responsibilities; supplying ethernet network connections (delivery services) and migration services. Those services are delivered to Corporate Market, Wholesale and Mobile. The project aimed to optimize the delivery services.

Core Roll-Out Delivery was initially comprised of 24 engineers and their important component of the departments work consists of providing a network design with an annual production of 30,000 designs. A network design is a customer order to a network- solution and configuration. Due to the complicated and labored production process, over 15 percent of the orders had to be redesigned and more than 10 percent of the order data was not clean, which led to an FTR of less than 70 percent. The lead time of a standard design before the project was five working days.

The priorities for Core Roll-Out Delivery were to:
1. Lower costs by using less FTE for the delivery services;
2. Improve customer satisfaction by increasing FTR to a minimum of 85 percent and reducing dirty data (achieving higher quality of order data);
3. Reduce the diversity in applications: this will serve to reduce the number of systems and applications and to simplify delivery and support, which result in lower costs;

4. Give the possibility of real-time provisioning (delivery) for internal customers (Corporate Market, Wholesale and Mobile) by creating zero-touch processes with advanced business ruling and high-end integration (process automation KPI of at least 85 percent).

4. THE KEY INNOVATIONS

The main innovation for Core Roll-Out Delivery (Operations) was to replace repetitive activities (manual tasks) performed by engineers with automated tasks using complex business rules combined with Business Process Management (BPM) software and advanced integration solutions.

To create chainwide zero-touch order processes, standardization of datasets and business decision making was important. The main innovation for IT was to create a sustainable IT-landscape based on a scalable orchestrator (BPM software) and a high-end integrator to control processes and applications.

The key innovations involved over 3,000 Business Rules to automate and control digital decisioning, validations and authorizations; these were based on four, mutually-beneficial goals:

o   To reduce workload (and costs);

o   To increase FTR and improve the quality of order data;

o   To simplify KPN Network and reduce the diversity in applications;

o   To accelerate provisioning and empower the end customer.

4.1 Business and Operational Impact

The project has had a substantial and direct impact on KPN Network Provider and internal customers (Corporate Market, Wholesale and Mobile), who are an active part in the supply chain process. With "Giving control to the end customer" in mind, the end customer benefited in multiple ways from the project outcomes.

KPN Network Provider

The project has had a major impact on the ethernet service delivery through the whole KPN supply chain, which involves hundreds of employees. The entire organization has standardized and optimized processes, minimizing response times, optimizing communication between users and reducing administrative / bureaucratic tasks to the absolute minimum, which has made it possible to focus on higher value-added tasks and positively and clearly impacting the end customer.

Internal Customer

The implementation has had a significant impact on internal customers (the business), given that all interaction with KPN Network Provider can now be carried out digitally using standard adapters for Corporate Market, Wholesale and Mobile. Without intervention from KPN Network Provider, internal customers are able to activate real-time ethernet and IP connectivity, standardize services and gain real-time monitoring.

End Customers

The end customer benefits directly and indirectly from the project outcomes. The direct benefits include the reduction in delivery times and a higher quality of services. The indirect benefits are the possibility to have greater control over the services delivered by KPN.

The achieved results are noteworthy, positively impacting operational efficiency, minimizing bureaucratic burden and improving service delivery time for the business. These were the business and operational impacts during the project:

o The customer service and quality are improved significantly by standardization of the services and eliminating human interaction, which can cause human errors;

o On a strategic level, the KPN network has been simplified;

o By standardizing order processes with business rules combined with the use of BPM software, KPN has achieved complete process traceability. As well all business rules and decision management, changes will be logged by the system and meet KPN's compliance requirements;

o Using business rules, instead of human intelligence, significantly improved efficiency due to the clarity, accessibility and reusability of business rules;

o Standardization of data throughout the chain has improved data quality. Because of the high quality of data, FTR has been improved significantly.

4.2 Innovation

When we take a closer look at the project's innovation, the three main innovations included the extensive use of business rules, the use of an enterprise service bus and the chain-wise use of BPM software.

1. To structure and eliminate inconsistent data in combination with managing authorization, integrity and behavioral business rules are used in three different ways:

   o Behavioral business rules on process decision level: Over 2,000 rules are used to make event-based decisions;

   o Integrity business rules on validation level: Over 1,000 rules are used to validate incoming and out-going data between applications;

   o Behavioral business rules on authorization level: depending on the services, users and systems; over 300 rules are used to manage authorizations.

   For the integration, the complexity of business rules has been drawn from Enterprise Service Bus to BPM software, this creates a more sustainable and flexible integration between software;

2. Using an Enterprise Service Bus (ESB) to structure communication between mutually interacting software applications in a service-oriented architecture (SOA);

3. Using BPM software for complex business process configuration and continuous improvement of business agility by using Business Process Lifecycle in combination with BPM software and Agile methodology.

4.3 Impact and Implementation

The project to automate the technical orchestration was completed in just 18 months. Within this time frame, a team of specialists was formed to design, develop and execute project improvements. Because all the stakeholders were involved in the project, decisions could be made, and issues were solved quickly. To make the project more manageable, the project was broken down into three phases:

o In the first phase, integration was developed with Network Management Systems;

o The second phase involved implementing business rules to eliminate repetitive activities and replace human intelligence;

o The final phase was linking these zero-touch processes to the Service Providers, using BPM software, high-end integration, business rules and decision management.

First phase:

At first, the project team started with the quick-wins in the current BPM software to create value for the stakeholders as quickly as possible. This involved the integration part with the Network Management Systems (back-end systems) to eliminate the copy paste work for engineers from Core Roll-Out Delivery (Operations). This resulted in:

o   Less workload for the department Core Roll-Out Delivery;
o   Different way of working for engineers, who were internally trained before each change;
o   Better understanding by system and enterprise Architects of data inconsistency between systems;
o   Better understanding by Process Managers how to design business rules;
o   Better understanding of decision management by Operations;
o   Better understanding by the project team how to standardize services throughout the whole chain.

Second phase:

The main goal of the second phase was to implement business rules to eliminate repetitive activities and replace human intelligence with business ruling. For each scenario Engineers from the Core Roll-Out Delivery department were interviewed to determine the best solution. Together with system and enterprise Architects and Process Managers, they decided in which system the data should be stored and how the business ruling should eliminate human interaction. Implementing business rules has resulted in:

o   Reduced workload for the Core Roll-Out Delivery department by eliminating human interaction and replacing it with advanced business ruling;
o   Improved knowledge management of the Core Roll-Out Delivery team, with work shift towards exception management. The team can now dedicate their time to focus on the tasks that add value;
o   Less errors, a higher FTR, better data quality and a significant workload reduction;
o   Greater understanding of how to create zero-touch processes for the next phase and connect them to the internal customers.

Third phase:

The last phase consisted of creating a zero-touch service delivery process, using BPM software, high-end integration and business rules to give the possibility for internal customers (Corporate Market, Wholesale and Mobile) to activate real-time ethernet and IP connectivity and gain real-time monitoring.

This resulted in:

o   Standardization of service data for all internal customers;
o   Elimination of human interaction (replaced with advanced business ruling);
o   Operations and internal customers focus on exception management;
o   Simplified processes and IT-landscape, empowering IT to adopt new services quickly (optimized time-to-market);
o   Increased visibility and traceability. Internal customers can monitor service orders within fulfilment;
o   Reduction of operational risks by giving structure to data and processes;

- o Minimized workload for Operations;
- o Optimized traceability of service orders throughout the whole chain.

5. HURDLES OVERCOME

5.1 Management

Because of the common goal; chainwide value creation and benefits for multiple departments, we received a lot of support from the management. Clear value creation and the direct interaction between Dev and Ops teams, helped the project to be successful. Any issues in terms of priority or assurance budgets were easily solved with the help of management teams chainwide. The approach we used is therefore just an example of how to be successful when working together to implement a project chainwide.

Maybe the biggest hurdle to overcome was getting the business-side (Service Provider) management to grasp the long-term and mind-shifting aspects of this innovation. To overcome this hurdle, we selected a digital platform with Agile methodology, thus, the project team delivered value to their stakeholders every four weeks. Within one month, the first Return on Value (RoV) was created for Core Roll-Out Delivery, which made it easier to apply for subsequent budget for each phase. Carefully selecting the order of process improvements helped to deliver fast RoV to get senior management onboard and realize the potential benefits. By building the improved processes and partial implementation, the business-side (management and operations) witnessed step by step of the usability and potency of this innovation.

5.2 Organization Adoption

The project team was formed thoughtfully, considering the challenge that production should be continued, and the customers should not notice the changes being made to the network. However, thanks to a very capable and coordinated multidisciplinary team (IT, KPN Network Provider, Core Roll-Out Delivery, internal customers and a variety of external collaborators) and Agile methodology, reengineered processes with advanced business rules were successfully digitalized.

KPN developed a work methodology with proven success in previous experiences, based on process development agility. It involves deploying the processes as fast as possible (initial version of minimum viable product) and making continuous improvements in subsequent versions. Each phase of the project involved training the engineers before each change, ensuring they were fully aware of the new way of working. Any initial reluctance to change soon vanished when the employees saw their workload decrease.

6. BENEFITS

Core Roll-Out Delivery was the initiator and funder of the project. By improving the network and standardizing order data and services, the business (internal customers) became aware of the benefits for themselves and for the end-customer.

6.1 Cost Savings / Time Reductions

Core Roll-Out Delivery provides three services:
- o Delivery service; design and activation;
- o Planning and support services;
- o Migration service; customer migration and standard migrations.

Over 2016 and 2017, the delivery services production volume remained stable with 30,000 designs per year. Project results led to substantial reduction in FTE for delivery services; design and activation. Resources were almost immediately deployed to accelerated customer migrations for network optimization (lifecycle management).

The graphic below shows how resources (FTE) within the Core Roll-Out Delivery department shifted from delivery services to migration services in 2016 and 2017 due to the high level of automation.

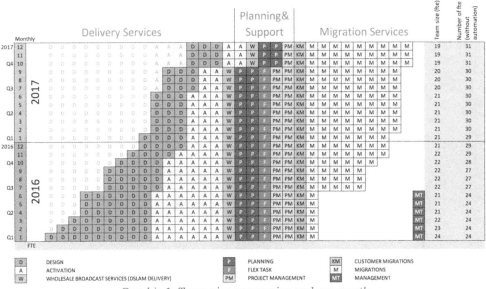

Graphic 1: Team size per service and per month

Although the duration of the project was 18 months, the results continued developing as old processes were phased out. Besides shifting the workload from delivery services to migration services, the team size was reduced from 24 FTE to 19 FTE.

Creating zero-touch processes, in combination with thousands of business rules, process automation increased from 21 percent to 98 percent and the delivery time to the business decreased drastically. The current team members working on delivery services are mainly focus on processing overdue orders, cleaning up data and supervising complex deliveries. By doing this, the FTR rose from <70 percent to >95 percent. In 2019, the team for delivery services will consist of 1 FTE.

Benefits summarized:
- o   Overall team size reduced from 24 FTE to 19 FTE in 2017;
- o   Delivery services team size reduces from 16 to 4 FTE in 2017;
- o   FTR rose from <70 percent to >95 percent;
- o   Delivery time from Core Roll-Out Delivery to business was reduced from 5 days to 10 minutes;
- o   Process automation increased from 21 percent to 98 percent.

6.2 Increased Revenues

The migration services grew considerably in 2016/2017. At the start of 2016, there were 80 migrations a month, which increased to 780 migrations a month at the end of 2017, all managed with a smaller team due to automating delivery services.

6.3 Quality Improvements

Benefits of phase 1:

Integration with the Network Management Systems eliminated the copy/paste tasks from one system to another. Because Engineers had to push the button manually for sending data between systems, the automation part for delivery service was just seven percent. With a baseline of 21 percent, after phase 1, 28 percent of the process was automated. The quality of the data improved significantly, because data validations managed by business ruling became standard process behavior, meaning less system contamination.

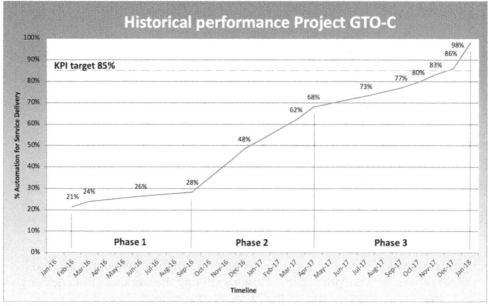

Graphic 2: Percentage of delivery service automation during the project

Benefits of phase 2:

The second phase involved implementing business rules to eliminate repetitive activities and replace human intelligence. Using more than 3,000 business rules, 40 percent of the process was automated. Another important benefit was the increasingly cleaner data in systems. After phase 2, the process automation went up to 68 percent.

Benefits of phase 3:

The final phase was creating and linking these zero-touch processes to the Service Providers. Because processes were standardized chainwide, the diversity in applications was reduced. This serves to reduce the number of systems and applications and to simplify delivery and support, which has been resulting in lower costs for Operations and IT. For the Business, real-time provisioning (delivery) was created and Engineers can now focus on exception management, instead of monitoring all processes.

Overall, the achieved results are remarkable, positively impacting fulfilment efficiency for Core Roll-Out Delivery (reduced workload and achieved process control and monitoring) and other areas, such as IT (simplifying IT-landscape and reducing risk by implementing a scalable orchestrator to control processes and applications), Internal Customers (higher FTR, standardized services and real-time monitoring).

7. BEST PRACTICES, LEARNING POINTS AND PITFALLS

7.1 Best Practices and Learning Points

✓ *Giving meaning to the project and driving enthusiasm within your team are the basic rules to be successful. The common goals, which were established chainwide, ensured that everyone who worked on the project, did their utmost to make the project successful;*

✓ *Implementation of the BPM based processes using Agile methodology, seeking to launch the Minimum Viable Service (MVS) as quickly as possible. The process can then be tested and adapted quickly to make all necessary changes. In addition, new versions of the processes can be presented, improving the current processes and including the less important cases in terms of strategic and operational impact, in a continuous improvement spiral;*

✓ *Identify and implement 'Quick Wins' detected in the diagnostic phase of the processes, although they do not solve the problems definitively (this is achieved through reengineering and digitalization using BPM software), they attenuate negative perceptions of the process implementation;*

✓ *Agile execution of tests and pilots, as an intermediate step towards the final development of the process, not consuming any more time than is strictly necessary;*

✓ *To have external collaborators who contribute their experience and manpower in key areas of implementation (process development, methodology and project management);*

✓ *It is important to implement a training plan (on-site training sessions, online training and manuals) as another element to eliminate the doubts of the users involved in the processes.*

7.2 Pitfalls

✗ *Arranging connectivity within a highly secure IT environment takes a lot of time and effort;*

✗ *Not be exhaustive in relation to all possible exceptions;*

✗ *Failure to understand which issues are indispensable in a first version and which, although not very repetitive, constitute non-negotiable requirements to consider from the beginning;*

✗ *Not launching processes until they are perfect, instead of later adjusting the potential errors (the devil is in the details);*

✗ *Failure to establish adequate prioritization in the processes, either because the operational and strategic relevance of the process is not understood or because the order is not developed logically.*

8. COMPETITIVE ADVANTAGES

The project goals will benefit not only KPN's corporate customers, but also KPN Wholesale. Wholesale is responsible for the delivery of services for external service providers such as T-Mobile and Vodafone. The same benefits apply for all three internal customers; Corporate Market, Wholesale and Mobile,

Thanks to the 'Business Rules implementation project', KPN has successfully developed the following competitive advantages:

o Reduced time to market;
o Transparency and standardization;
o Promote and support the FTR strategy, naturally driving efficiency and boosting customer satisfaction;

- o Optimal use of human resources, with employees shifting their focus to tasks that require human interaction and intelligence;
- o High level of automation with advanced business rules has empowered KPN to reduce SLAs from five days to ten minutes for delivery time from Core Roll-Out delivery to business.

9. TECHNOLOGY

The Core Roll-Out Delivery department is process driven. This means that the department continually optimizes their process, working to become extremely efficient while maintaining value. As a foundation for orchestrating business processes, Core Roll-Out Delivery uses a BPM software with an integrated business rule management module. In addition to the orchestrating tool, high-end integration (Enterprise Service Bus) connects all necessary systems to the orchestrating BPM software in a Service-Oriented Architecture (SOA).

For this project, an advanced orchestrator connects the Business Support Systems (BSS) to the Operational Support Systems (OSS). By automating decisioning, using business rule management and standardized data, the business can use zero-touch provisioning. This enables the people from Operations closest to the rules to participate directly in managing the logic.

The unique benefit for the business is to increase the time-to-market for new revenue opportunities or changes to existing services. Orchestrating systems and applications by using BPM software and business rule management allows Operations to make changes, which are beneficial to the business, without support from IT. By giving more structure to IT, using Agile methodology, IT can make decision-management changes in a short period of time, which expedite the business' time-to-market.

10. THE TECHNOLOGY AND SERVICE PROVIDERS

The four external collaborators in the project were:

AuraPortal:

Digital Business Platform for the design and execution of operational processes using BPM software with a powerful Business Rules Engine. The implemented AuraPortal BPM Suite automatically controls parts of operations from the beginning to end, or specific organizational areas. The development of the processes and integration solutions was carried out by FourICT and KPN AuraPortal Team.

For more information: https://www.auraportal.com

FourICT:

A consultancy firm specializing in digitalization with strong integration and IT solutions, from the definition of the digital vision to its implementation, guaranteeing a successful digital transformation, always focusing on tangible and achievable results in the short and medium term. FourICT is official EMEA (implementation) Partner of AuraPortal.

For more information: http://www.fourict.nl/contact/

Tech Mahindra:

A leading global systems integrator and advisor in the field of business transformation, mainly focused on the telecommunications sector. Tech Mahindra provides services to telecom companies, telecommunication equipment manufacturers and independent software vendors and is a valued partner in transforming several leading fixed, mobile and broadband providers in Europe, Asia / Pacific and North America.

For more information: https://www.techmahindra.com/

Nokia:

A global leader in innovations such as mobile networks, digital health and phones. Nokia has long-standing relationships with CSPs, including fixed, mobile, converged and cable network operators, located around the world. Our solutions help transform our customers' business and their networks. Through our comprehensive portfolio of hardware, software and services we enable the digital transformation of networks to address capacity needs, reduce complexity and leverage network intelligence to create and deliver new services.

For more information: https://www.nokia.com/

MMG Insurance, USA
by EA Department, MMG Insurance, USA

1. EXECUTIVE SUMMARY / ABSTRACT

Three years ago, MMG Insurance began a business transformation journey involving legacy system replacement and a customer-facing portal modernization. MMG's future growth plan required that the technology platform supporting MMG's core business processes be robust, agile, and scalable. In partnership with our core system vendor and several third parties, we completed the first part of this journey in February 2018; with the replacement of our billing system.

Challenges came with our core system vendor having teams offshore in India and others in the US. Conflicting terminology was used amongst internal and vendor teams, and management of rules varied. Miscommunication occurred, whether face-to-face, during conference calls, or in hand-offs of documentation.

To combat this, we leaned on our dedication to managing rules and terminology in a consistent, business-friendly, and shareable way, by using a business rule management tool to create a single source of truth. Effective business rule and terminology management was instrumental in MMG being fully operational on day one.

2. OVERVIEW

The deliverable of the first phase of MMG's business transformation initiative was the billing system replacement. The billing system was chosen as the first core system to replace because billing is one of the most critical functions to the company. It provides a means to manage billing accounts, generate invoices, apply fees, manage insurance agency commissions, and most importantly, collect money and process premium payments. In order to support growth goals, it was important that the new billing system enabled such billing functions to be performed effectively and efficiently, as well as allow for quick and easy modification of system configuration to meet evolving business needs.

Due to the time and effort involved with such a project, MMG decided to buy versus build. Despite this, there was still an extensive amount of work to do. Billing impacted many areas of the business including accounting, customer service, underwriting, and marketing. Between MMG and the core system vendor, there were nine development teams dedicated to the project, as well as several sub-teams that tackled specific pockets of work associated with third-party integrations. As a result of the complexity of the work, the amount of coordination required across parties, and the lack of agreed upon business vocabulary, communicating and sharing of information was very challenging. Context-setting and aligning were a focus of nearly every meeting to ensure everyone was on the same page. This became a need with co-located teams at MMG, core system vendor teams in India, and third parties across the world. It was common for misunderstandings to occur due to inconsistent communication methods and basic misinterpretations. Another significant hurdle to overcome was the lack of a single source of billing-related business vocabulary and business rules. Since existing billing capabilities were enabled through legacy systems and applications, no formal analysis had been performed on them. This meant very few billing-related concepts and business rules were captured.

In response, we leveraged our established business rule approach to manage terms and business rule across parties. We aligned MMG and vendor terminology into a single enterprise model, using synonyms as reference sources. We linked MMG and vendor business rules by adding vendor rule name as a custom property in our business rule management tool. In turn, change agents used this to develop trainings. Data conversion leveraged this to enable appropriate mapping and validation for moving data between systems. Developers used this as the basis for user interface elements, messages, and automated test cases. Quality Analysts executed test coverage whose accuracy benefited from this single source.

Upon the billing release, MMG employees were fully trained on all relevant changes and user experience and workflow were enhanced. Results for data conversion and quality assurance were well above average for core system replacement projects. Over 400,000 records had been converted with 99.99 percent accuracy and QA achieved a 96 percent defect containment rate.

3. Business Context

When rationalizing future growth plans against MMG's current state, it became apparent that legacy processes, systems, and applications would be major inhibitors in realizing growth and scaling goals. Existing legacy systems were not built to accommodate such a significant transformation. Due to system complexities, product flexibility was limited and speed to market was not as fast as needed. The ability for employees to work, sell, and service from anywhere was restricted since systems were not designed to handle this. Without automated alerts and notifications, turnaround times of customer and insurance agent services were at risk of going long. Addressing modern consumer expectations through mobile, web, and other emerging technologies became an afterthought, as the work to integrate with legacy systems was quite complicated. Eliminating IT involvement from something as simple as workflow and task management for a given business domain was impossible due to various complexities. Because of system constraints, providing dependable information to enable good business decisions was difficult. Lastly and most alarmingly, legacy systems were just not built to support projected growth, leading to considerable scalability issues.

4. The Key Innovations

4.1 Business and Operational Impact

Part of MMG's mission is to provide exceptional customer service through well-trained, professional employees armed with cutting edge technology. Replacing the billing system was the first major step toward this, and since going live with the billing system there have been many positive results, and more to be expected over time.

Operationally, the organization enhanced its customer service by having many individuals knowledgeable in billing functions. Prior to the billing implementation, there were only a few billing experts and the ability to update and maintain the system was restricted to just a couple people. Now, there are several experts across all business domains. When an insurance customer calls a customer service representative or an insurance agent calls an underwriter, they can expect to get billing inquiries and issues resolved quickly and comprehensively. This represents an improvement in overall quality of MMG service. Having multiple people versed in billing vocabulary, processes, and customer concerns led to a reliable and consistent customer experience.

From a customer retention perspective, the use of a modern billing system enabled product flexibility, specifically by providing additional billing and payment options for insurance customers. For example, in the previous system, payment plans were restricted because insurance policies were invoiced together. Now, policyholders have the option to select a payment plan per insurance policy. Additionally, due dates were limited to just a few days of the month.

Now, policyholders can choose any day between 1 and 28. Externally, providing a quick and simple way for insurance agents to sell and service MMG policies was and remains a top priority. This aligns with an enterprise goal to support the health and sustainability of our agency relationships. That being said, MMG's agency portal experienced transformation also. Various user interfaces that included billing-related information were revamped to have a modern look and feel. Furthermore, similar changes were applied to the insured portal to ensure a consistent user experience. In both cases, end-users participated in valuable usability sessions that allowed us to directly observe portal use and capture feedback.

Another enterprise goal enabled through the billing initiative is managing the total cost of ownership of business capabilities. Early on, MMG decided to leverage vendor systems and services for commodity functions, but to also build and internally maintain systems that provide differentiation in the market with insurance agents, policyholders, and prospects. The billing system fell into the former tactic, while agency and policyholder portals fell into the latter. Whether it was buying or building systems, MMG was able to utilize a business rule approach, ensuring consistent use of business language and implementation of business rules. Following a business rule approach led to consistent and positive outcomes across development teams and the organization.

Due to the size and complexity of this core system replacement, it was imperative to have adequate business vocabulary and rules governance. Because many billing functions span multiple business domains, it is important that we had a common understanding of concepts and business rules. When we ran into a concept that had not been modeled previously or was not modeled sufficiently, the concept model process was initiated. Concept models were developed by a Business Analyst (BA) and reviewed by an Enterprise Language Steward and Enterprise Data Steward. This ensured appropriate modeling and structure of concepts. Next, domain subject matter experts (SMEs) reviewed and formally approved the concept model, terms, and term definitions. As far as business rules and decisions were concerned, a BA initially gathered the information needed to write business rules. This involved analyzing documents, working with SMEs, or a combination of both. Next, the BA drafted business rules and marked them as *proposed*. Then, the BA would meet with a peer to have a review done. The peer ensured that the business rules followed patterns, standards, and leveraged appropriate business vocabulary. Finally, the BA reviewed the business rules with SMEs for approval. Upon approval, the business rules were marked *approved* with the SMEs listed accordingly.

4.2 Innovation

Business rules and decisions were directly associated to vendor business rules and decisions through the use of custom properties in our business rule management tool. The view of the *Lookup Minimum Billable Amount* business rule came from the business rule web portal, which allowed organization-wide access to business rules, decisions, terminology, and concept models. In our core system vendor's insurance content management system, there were two business rules associated, one called *Minimum Amount for Invoicing* and the other called *Minimum Amount for Invoicing By Payment Method*. We were able to take two business rules and consolidate them into a single rule, which made it easier for stakeholders to consume. Additionally, this rule was in agreed upon business language, which made it relevant and simple to understand. A major project

Lookup Minimum Billable Amount
Rule3798

status: operational

The minimum billable amount must be as in the minimum billable amount table for a given kind of payment method.

Reference Source:
   Reference Source URL: Click to open in a new tab
Informal: No
ICM Rule Name: Minimum Amount for Invoicing, Minimum Amount for Invoicing By Payment Method

kind of payment method	minimum billable amount
invoice payment method	$10
EFT payment method	$2

stakeholder, and consumer of this information, was the change agent. Change agents represented specific business domains and were tasked with learning about changes, becoming experts on them, and training others. In many cases, change agents leveraged business rules, decisions, and terminology captured in the business rule management tool to facilitate self-learning, develop training material for respective business domains, and accelerate the adoption of change.

Another important activity was reconciling MMGs terminology against the terminology of third parties. Our core system vendor had an existing glossary of hundreds of terms that we were able to import it into the business rule management tool. To quickly distinguish these terms from MMG's, a suffix was added (- *XYZ* in the example below). This enabled developers, change agents, business analysts, quality analysts, architects, product owners, and many others

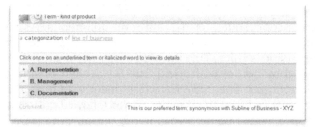

Term - kind of product

a categorization of line of business

Click once on an underlined term or italicized word to view its details

* A. Representation
* B. Management
* C. Documentation

Comment   This is our preferred term; synonymous with Subline of Business - XYZ

to look up terms "on demand" when they were used, limiting miscommunication and confusion. This was particularly useful when an MMG term and a third-party term were listed as completely different terms yet meant the same. For example, we have a term *kind of product* defined as *a categorization of line of business*. On the other hand, our core system vendor used the term *subline of business*, which aligned with our *kind of product* term and definition. The resolution was adding subline of business as a synonym of kind of product, with kind of product being our preferred term.

4.3 Impact and Implementation

The billing system implementation impacted the entire company. Across all business domains, there are now more people versed in billing than ever before. Sub-groups formed within various business domains specialized on certain billing functions, enabling more efficient responses and resolutions to inquiries and issues. Change agents assigned to domains were able to learn billing changes, acquire deep billing knowledge, train others, and be available to help once operational with the new system. Territory Managers, who maintain independent insurance agency relationships, were trained on all the billing changes that were impactful to insurance agents and policyholders. Those Territory Managers no longer had to rely solely on Customer Service and Underwriting to field and answer questions, as they now have the knowledge to be self-sufficient. However, more complex questions led to more collaboration between business domains, which enhanced working and interpersonal relationships. Accounting expanded their knowledge of billing functions providing versatility when it comes to job duties and responsibilities. Overall, the increase of billing knowledge significantly reduced the enterprise's risk of having all billing expertise held by just a couple people. In the past, if MMG's billing experts were not available, a billing issue could result in many insurance policies being placed on-hold and the prevention of premium processing for a detrimental period of time. To put this into perspective, transactions total over $850,000 per day in payments and refunds across nearly 1,400 insurance policies. Today, MMG is prepared with an extensive team of billing experts available to triage and tackle issues promptly and efficiently.

From the view of a developer, following a business rule approach made things simpler. First, having outputs exposed through a business rules web portal saved development teams countless hours by providing unrestricted access to term definitions and relationships between terms, concept models, and business rules. This allowed developers to easily determine which business rules needed to be implemented, and which concept models needed to be applied in order to complete a given product backlog item. Translating these outputs into working code was quick because of how effective and efficiently they had been exposed through the business rule web portal. Overall, using a business rule management tool allowed the organization to achieve great efficiency in developing complex software systems. Second, automated acceptance tests were written using business language. This meant anyone on the development team or SMEs from the business could review and understand what the test was trying to accomplish. Furthermore, business rules were referenced, via rule identifiers, to provide traceability. If there was a question on a given business rule, the reviewer of the test could simply look up the rule in the portal to find exactly what they needed. This approach to automated acceptance testing ensured the proper implementation of business rules and use of business language. Lastly, the dedication to consistent use of terminology across screens and messages allowed for a more intuitive experience, whereby the user knew exactly what they were looking at and why. Terminology used for labels, drop down values, and other elements on user interfaces matched business language captured in concepts models and our enterprise glossary. Validation rules that were invoked resulted in violation messages that followed patterns and leveraged business language. The rule *Check Insurance Billing Account has Payment Method* was an example. In general, working through terminology gaps led to collaboration across the organization, vendors, and third parties. This helped establish a consistent, well-understood set of business vocabulary and business rules.

> **Check Insurance Billing Account has Payment Method**
> Rule3763
> status: operational
>
> An insurance billing account must have exactly one payment method.
>
> **Violation Message:**
> "A payment method is required."

MMG being fully operational on day 1 after the billing system release would not have been the case without an emphasis on quality. As previously mentioned, developers wrote code against business rules and decisions and inherently embedded business vocabulary. Test cases followed suit by using business language and referencing business rules. This provided consistency and quality results across business artifacts, including concept models, business rules, and decisions, technical architecture, and test cases. As shown to the right, the test case references the business rule identifier and uses the same business language as used in the prior example business rule *Lookup Minimum Billable Amount*. Additionally,

having business rules and terminology easily accessible via the business rule web portal enabled effective verification by quality analysts and business testers. In the end, QA achieved a 96 percent defect containment rate, also known as 4 percent defect leakage. This was a very positive result, as the average for similar core system replacement projects is 90-92 percent containment, with anything greater than 95 percent being very difficult, according to MMG's software testing augmentation consultant.

From a data perspective, the billing implementation resulted in MMG's most significant transformation of data ever. Moving data from the legacy system to the new system required extensive planning, coordination, and collaboration. The data conversion team excelled due to a variety of factors, one being the capture of corporate knowledge and business vocabulary. Several concepts had to be understood, defined, modeled, mapped, and validated. For example, insurance billing account was a concept utilized by the new billing system, but a new concept for MMG. Because this was a standard language in the insurance industry, MMG chose to adopt, define, and concept model it. In turn, the data conversion team had clearly defined terms and business rules to reference. All the planning, coordination, and collaboration culminated in MMG converting over two years of data composed of over 400,000 billing records from the legacy billing system to the new billing system. This was accomplished with 99.99 percent accuracy, as only one record failed during conversion.

5. HURDLES OVERCOME

5.1 Management

Flying a plane while building it is the metaphor that has been used to describe keeping the business operational while replacing core systems at the same time. From a management perspective, this presented an extensive challenge. Managers from each department had to determine how to best accommodate the billing system replacement in terms of workloads and training. Each department had one or more change agents dedicated to the project that resulted in a shift of job duties. As training ramped up, managing workloads and work assignments became more complex. The work that change agents would typically do shifted to others within the department. For a department like Customer Service, where phone calls with insurance customers are frequent, scheduling training required careful coordination. Managers also had to consider if everyone would be trained on everything, or only trained on specific billing functions or processes. Through guidance from the Change Management Lead and collaboration across change agents, each department was able to develop a plan that worked for them, both for the short- and long-terms. In many cases, small pockets of employees were trained in a specific area to enable a short learning curve and lessen the impact on operational work due to minimalized time away from their workspaces.

5.2 Business

During the billing implementation, we encountered a substantial communication challenge. We were collaborating with people from around the globe. Our core system vendor had product and implementation teams located in India, while other team members are located in New York and onsite at MMG. We partnered with two software testing augmentation providers that had an offshore testing team in India and individual testers onsite. Third parties, which we integrated with, were spread out across the United States, from California to Florida. Lastly, we had a large contingent of independent insurance agents across 503 insurance agency offices in Maine, New Hampshire, Vermont, Pennsylvania, and Virginia to consider.

Due to differences in location, language, and terminology across all parties, it was not uncommon for miscommunication to occur, whether talking face-to-face, interpreting documentation, or during conference calls. Team members in India were 9.5 hours ahead of us, therefore communication was difficult at times. There was heavy reliance on email and documents being passed back and forth. If offshore teams ran into issues in the middle of their work day, we were not available. On the other hand, when in the middle of our work day, offshore teams were not available. In some cases, we talked about things that we thought both sides had the same understanding of, but actually did not. This led to longer conversations and multiple revisions of configuration documents. To overcome the communication, terminology, and business rule challenges, we needed a single source of rules and terminology across all parties. Fortunately, we already had a solution in place for this problem. In past initiatives, we found success in leveraging a business rule management tool as our single source for business rules and enterprise terminology. For the billing initiative, we decided to double down on our business rule approach and capture all pertinent billing terms, business rules, and decisions. This resulted in over a dozen new concept models, and hundreds of new terms and business rules.

5.3 Organization Adoption

During development, there was a massive emphasis placed on change management. By talking with other insurers that went through core system replacement projects, MMG learned that ineffective change management can be disastrous. In response, a Change Management Lead was assigned to the project. Change agents were identified and assigned responsibility for understanding changes, developing and providing training on the changes, and adjusting business domain workflows to accommodate the changes. A regular session to discuss change at a high level took place with business managers and supervisors. This kept key stakeholders and decision makers informed. A mission control

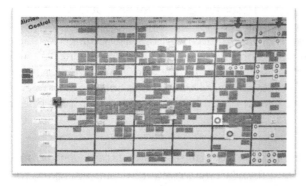

board, shown to the left, was created on a large wall in the building that allowed the sharing of project team, testing, and change agent updates. The change agent group, along with the lead Business Analyst and Product Owner of the project, met regularly to discuss what areas to focus on and what tasks were needed. This team approach was beneficial, as questions about changes could be discussed together, yielding a common understanding. Additionally, change agents were able to leverage each other's training content and material for their own trainings. The Business Analyst kept change agents informed of enterprise terminology, business rules, and decisions captured to promote a shared understanding of changes. Change agents held trainings with their respective business domains. Many incorporated games, contests, and other fun ways to help with the adoption of organizational change.

6. BENEFITS

6.1 Cost Savings / Time Reductions

MMG is realizing, or on track to realize, lower maintenance costs, reduced time to market, enhanced ease of upgradeability, enhanced ease of scalability, and decreased time to stand up new environments. By following a business rule approach and leveraging core system development tools, we expect to see less time and effort dedicated to maintaining systems. Many of the legacy applications that we had were complex and required an extensive amount of time to change and test. In some cases, there was only a single developer who knew how to modify the application code or only a single tester who knew how to test. Now, with the billing system and other new applications, there will be concept models, terms, business rules, and decisions for everyone involved to reference and utilize during updates. Multiple developers will be able to make required changes, while multiple testers will be able to test required changes. This introduces significant flexibility and agility for the organization. The same applies to speed to market, upgradability, scalability, and time to stand up new environments. Code and test cases are written leveraging structured business vocabulary and well-written business rules and decisions. Having such business architecture to lean on and reuse during product changes or expansion into new markets bodes well for the organization and enhances the speed of implementation.

6.2 Increased Revenues

Prior to the billing implementation, legacy system constraints made it challenging to realize some revenue opportunities that any typical insurance company would expect. Many companies offer great flexibility around billing, including payment due date, payment frequency, and payment method. MMG, on the other hand, did not have such flexibility, which became a factor in insurance policies going into cancellation for non-payment. With the new system, policyholders are able to pay when they want and how they want. In turn, MMG collects premium as expected and as earned. If premium is not paid on time, the new billing system provides a way to handle that appropriately through equity-based cancellation. Due to legacy system constraints, the company had no way to collect premium on coverage that was provided and, as a result, premium was written off. With the billing implementation, equity-based cancellation was established, and policyholders are receiving an earned premium invoice with a final amount due. Therefore, premium will be paid for the coverage provided, unlike MMG's prior state.

6.3 Quality Improvements

With the billing release, MMG implemented a modern system while replacing a legacy system that was perceived by some to be dangerous and scary. Having a system take care of tasks that had to previously be done manually is a big boost for employees and their quality of work. Instead of focusing on trivial aspects of policy administration, underwriting, or accounting, employees can focus on the value-adds in each of those areas and provide exceptional, customer-oriented service.

A key success factor in this realm was our change management approach. Change agents from each business domain became experts on the billing changes, resulting in MMG having many billing experts compared to just a few before the implementation. This helped employees with making quality decisions during business processes, as everyone had a resource available to assist with billing issues, concerns, and workflow. Lastly, whether it is a change agent, customer service representative, underwriter, or accountant, everyone had a single source of truth of business vocabulary, business rules, and decisions. Further dedication to a business rule approach represents a quality improvement in and of itself. As previously mentioned, a small number of billing terms and business rules were captured before the billing implementation. Even though we had several base concepts that were extended to meet some of our billing needs from a business vocabulary perspective, we still created 22 new concept models and modified 13 existing concept models, resulting in 503 new terms. Additionally, 768 terms were imported from our core system vendor's glossary. Except for some existing business rules related to banking payments, we had no billing-related business rules. By the end of the billing implementation, we had captured 268 business rules and 90 decisions.

7. BEST PRACTICES, LEARNING POINTS AND PITFALLS

7.1 Best Practices and Learning Points

- ✓ Align on business terminology early across all parties involved in the implementation.
- ✓ Establish a single source of truth for terminology and business rules that is accessible and understandable to all parties involved in the implementation.
- ✓ Leverage a single source of truth for terminology and business rules for training and other change management activities.
- ✓ Keep as many communication channels open as possible.
- ✓ Write business rules using structured business vocabulary.
- ✓ Use decision tables as often as possible instead of writing individual rules with the same inputs.
- ✓ Leverage process modeling and policy charters to elicit and extract business rules.

7.2 Pitfalls

- ✗ *Assuming you are speaking the same business language.*
- ✗ *Not having adequate governance or oversight over a business rule approach.*

- × *Having too many "cooks in the kitchen" when reviewing business terms and rules for approval.*
- × *Capturing all new business terms and rules you think you will need in the beginning of the project.*
- × *Capturing business terms and rules that have little or no business value.*
- × *Capturing system rules as business rules.*

8. COMPETITIVE ADVANTAGES

MMG's high-tech, high-touch strategy is critical to execute successfully, considering the insurance industry is rapidly evolving in terms of how technology and customer experience are managed. InsurTech is changing the game and many insurers will not be in position to take advantage of these technologies due to legacy system constraints. This was a primary motivator for MMG to take on core system replacement. By enhancing core systems and modernizing customer-facing portals, MMG will gain internal efficiencies and enhance customer experience. Speed to market represents one of the most significant competitive advantages. Implementing product changes in response to market opportunities or expanding into new states will happen faster than ever.

9. TECHNOLOGY

The core system vendor managed business rules and list of values in an insurance content management system. Business rules were captured via decision tables and Drools. On the other hand, MMG business analysts managed a matching set of business rules and decisions following semantics of business vocabulary and rules (SBVR) and MMG-specific business rule patterns. Core system vendor developers managed UI design and flow in an insurance content designer, leveraged SOAP for web services, and revamped the billing system with HTML5. MMG developers leveraged C# and .NET framework, TypeScript, SCSS, HTML5, PowerShell, Chef, REST, OpenAPI, OAuth 2.0, and OpenID Connect. Automated testing tools were used by both parties. MMG utilized Gherkin in "given-when-then" format to write automated acceptance tests. As previously mentioned, these tests were written using business vocabulary, and validated the implementation of business rules and decisions. MMG plans to continue using a business rule approach for all subsequent phases of this business transformation initiative in order to provide the same level of traceability and transparency across project teams.

10. THE TECHNOLOGY AND SERVICE PROVIDERS

The core system vendor of the billing system implemented was Majesco. The business rule management tool leveraged throughout the project was RuleXpress, a product by RuleArts. Other technology and service providers included Office of Foreign Assets Control (OFAC) compliance software, payment gateway service, payment card industry (PCI) compliant hosting provider, insurance accounting system and software, data exchange software, document fulfillment vendor, and software testing augmentation providers.

PowerHealth, Australia
Nominated by IDIOM Limited, New Zealand

1. EXECUTIVE SUMMARY / ABSTRACT

PowerHealth (Australia) [PHS] provides its PowerPerformance Manager [PPM] and PowerBilling and Revenue Collection [PBRC] applications to healthcare organizations worldwide as Commercial Off the Shelf [COTS] applications.

PHS started a rules initiative that is the subject of this case study, with the objective of making costing/revenue and billing rules a plug-n-play feature within their applications. The separation of rules from the underlying applications was required to allow PHS to support bespoke customer rules within their otherwise standard applications.

A national client, with over 40 hospitals and more than 100 clinics, tendered for a new enterprise-wide billing application to span their 27,000 bed and 65,000 staff organisation, with an annual budget of USD 10B. The client had previously developed an in-house billing system that provided excellent functionality. However, ten years later, this system was proving difficult to maintain due to the billing logic being hard-coded within the software program code; meaning that changes had to be implemented by programmers. In addition, the technology platform used to develop the software was fast becoming obsolete.

The current PowerBilling and Revenue Collection (PBRC) application was built in response to the tender and extended the scale and complexity of the rules then under management by PHS. When complete, PBRC provided a new rules-driven billing capability on the global market for enterprise health billing solutions, which was at the time dominated by heavily siloed, departmental scale solutions.

Since the adoption of the rules initiative as described by this case study, PHS has expanded its footprint in its Australasian home market and expanded into overseas markets to include customers in the UK/Europe, the Middle East, South East Asia, and North America.

This submission uses the development of PBRC for this tender as a reference project for the initiative, to highlight the benefits of using rules as a formal architectural component within COTS applications.

2. OVERVIEW

The subject of this case study is the PowerHealth (Australia) [PHS] rules initiative, which separated and promoted the use of rules within their COTS applications, supported by the additional specific discussion around a single reference project that demonstrates key elements of the initiative.

The initiative is a key pillar of PHS's go-to-market strategy – it offers PHS's customers' autonomy in the management of their business rules while also claiming the benefits of a COTS application. To achieve this, the COTS application is fundamentally refactored to include an interface to the rules' engine, but no rules. The rules are then supplied on demand independently of the application itself.

The primary focus of the PHS rules is to convert raw patient encounter data into cost/revenue and billing data for the PPM and PBRC applications.

While the explicit focus of each of these applications is slightly different, the rules approach is consistent across the two applications. The separation of rules from the underlying applications allows PHS to provide bespoke costing/revenue and billing calculations from the otherwise standard applications.

Rules autonomy for the customer is flexible, with technology included within the rules toolset that provides an option for the customer to use PHS's rules, or to use the customer's own rules, either alone or in combination at any level of complexity. Both sets of rules, that is, PHS-supplied rules and the customer's own rules, can be updated independently, so that rule sharing is complete and ongoing.

Using this technology, PHS can provide a baseline, pre-configured rules that can be modified or added to by the customer (generally a hospital), who owns and manages the rules ongoing. Autonomous sets of rules can also be delegated to specialist departments throughout the enterprise, which is then dynamically re-acquired by the application and executed via the interface within the PHS defined rules topology, to achieve enterprise-wide coordination of discrete sets of rules within a single enterprise-wide process.

This approach required initial development and understanding of a rules topology, which was a critical outcome of the Project

The customer benefits and cost advantages of plug-n-play rules have helped PHS to become one of the world's largest suppliers of health costing/revenue and billing software, with expansion in its scope of operations since the rules initiative to the UK/Europe, the Middle East, South East Asia, and North America.

The reference Project for this submission is a national client with a requirement for enterprise scale billing system encompassing 40+ hospitals and 100+ clinics, and over 60,000 staff. This project exemplifies the advantages of the approach. Since the implementation of the new billing system, the client has claimed improvements in business agility, managing enterprise-wide variations in business practice, and managing complexity and performance, while processing 1,650,000 invoice items in real-time to generate 4,000 invoices per day at the point of care.

3. BUSINESS CONTEXT

PHS was established in 1995 with an innovative mission to build horizontal customer-centric applications rather than the vertical service or departmental centric applications that were then typical of the health market. The difference is significant – one billing platform instead of many; one bill instead of many; and enterprise-wide access to unified costing/revenue and billing data, rather than discrete siloed viewpoints on an application by application basis.

With customers in Australia and New Zealand, PHS recognized the advantages of using a rules approach: to manage the wide variety of cost input systems; to build a neutral middle-tier cost and revenue concept model; and ultimately to output unified costs, revenues, and invoices to service the wide variety of destination viewpoints required.

When a national tender for a new billing system was issued, PHS found that the client vision matched closely with PHS's vision for enterprise-wide billing. At that time, PHS was the only vendor able to represent this concept and was uncontested within the client's prime vendor shortlist.

The proposed new PBRC rules-centric billing application was selected. This required PHS to scale its rules approach to a new level, to span 40+ hospitals and 100+ clinics within a single billing system for consolidated enterprise-wide, real-time billing.

The requirements sought by the client at this time included the following:

- ### Business agility

The hardcoded business logic of the incumbent in-house developed system proved extremely difficult to change in response to new business requirements. As the client's business practice is driven by external demand and government policy, it is imperative that new policies and policy changes can be actioned quickly.

- ### Enterprise-wide

The old system was hospital- and episode-based and deployed as separate standalone systems at each hospital/clinic. Where a patient presented at more than one hospital or was transferred between hospitals, they were recorded under different IDs with no data sharing among locations. As the client wanted to move to an enterprise-wide patient-based system, the only practical option was to replace the old system.

- ### Variations in business practice

Although the same core software was deployed across the organization, each instance operated independently and according to individual facilities' preferred billing processes. Invoices were branded with hospital identities and not the organization brand. Each system maintained separate patient records, and service codes were also interpreted inconsistently.

- ### Complexity

The client's billing policy requires complex decision making based on many factors. The in-house development was struggling to meet these requirements. It was therefore a top priority that the replacement software could handle both the complexity and need for regular change without constant enhancements to the underlying program code.

- ### Performance

To operate effectively, the client's billing model required a patient facing system that provides fast turnaround in order to issue invoices and collect payment at time of service. Time taken by the billing system to generate an invoice while the patient is waiting is therefore vitally important, particularly during peak periods.

From a rules' perspective, both PBRC and PPM have the need to transform large numbers of raw cost events for each patient encounter into intermediate forms before generation of invoice line items or service delivery costs/revenues, respectively.

An encounter refers to a period of treatment, more or less from admission to discharge. For the sake of clarity, the encounter refers to the period rather than the treatment, so that one encounter may include many treatments. This subtle distinction is important because the various treatments may require multiple sets of discrete funding rules from a variety of funding parties that may overlap. Partially for this reason, the rules need to transform the inbound cost factors into more or less neutral concepts before re-collating them by funder/funding agreement. At this point, cost sharing and allocation rules may add significant complexity.

For instance, consider a patient having a private knee operation who has heart failure during anaesthesia; which funding agreement pays what in these circumstances? Until discharged, this constitutes one encounter, and for in-patients, this can be an extended period (usually days, but extending to years in some cases).

The input costs span many medical and support disciplines, while the revenue is likely to be derived from multiple funding agreements, both public and private.

In each case, raw medical and administrative 'factors' that describe the consumption of the health provider's resources are acquired by electronically receiving messages from a wide variety of clinical and administrative systems. The totality of these messages includes all data required to calculate correct costs and charges according to defined rules, and may include service codes, ward transfer details to calculate time spent in wards and other locations, and/or data coded using industry coding systems such as DRG & ICD.

These raw message items need to be transformed into a neutral, schema-defined format. Some of these costs are attributed directly (e.g. a service is provided) or they may be apportioned indirectly (e.g. overhead for a particular ward stay based on presence in the ward), often on an hour-by-hour basis.

These items then need to be transformed into cost, revenue, and/or billing values in accordance with the contract rules in multiple funding agreements. Meta rules regarding shared funding capped funding, and other cross-contract aggregation or apportioning also need to be applied, which can add significant complexity.

These rules come from different sources, including PHS themselves, the hospital organization, and the multitude of public and private funding agencies. Often, the funding contracts are the same or similar across hospital organizations, providing an additional opportunity for sharing of rules.

Coding each hospital's rules from scratch is expensive and time-consuming. PHS, therefore, seeks to provide rule supersets that provide an estimated complete set of rules for adjustment and tailoring during the implementation process. By using a rules engine to achieve this, the application is relieved of responsibility for managing these rules. In fact, the PHS applications are not aware of the rules they contain – they are only aware of the specific outputs that are generated at the conclusion of each rules cycle. This means that one COTS application image can manage the cost/revenue and/or billing rules respectively for any and all hospitals across multiple jurisdictions.

In summary, the rules engine must manage a complex set of transformations at scale, to ultimately apply a complex set of rules representing multiple parties while maximizing the reuse of rules on a global basis.

4. THE KEY INNOVATIONS

4.1 Business and Operational Impact

The PHS Initiative

Using a rules engine that accepts rules from multiple sources (both internal and external) and which executes them as a contiguous set has allowed PHS to offer an agile and cost-effective solution to its customers worldwide. By normalizing and reusing rules at many levels, including global rules, jurisdictional rules, rules per funding contract, and rules for each and every cost center in the hospital, PHS has been able to reduce the investment required to convert cost items into cost/revenue and/or invoice line items in accordance with funding contracts and the hospitals own cost accounting procedures.

This has led to increased sales, and ultimately, global expansion.

The Project

This project exemplifies the benefits of the initiative described above. In the first year of operation, the metrics included more than 20 million encounters, with nearly two million inbound cost messages per day resulting in several thousand invoices being presented in real-time at the point of discharge per day.

The validation and transformation of these cost elements required unique algorithms for each specialist department. There are 26 distinct decision models operating in concert to achieve unified, enterprise-wide billing.

The result is fine-grained variation in rules while maximizing reuse on a large scale.

In achieving this business objective and throughput, substantial complexity was addressed. In business terms, some examples include:

Radiology weighting rules

Using PBRC's business rules engine, the client can group radiology charges by order number and modality and apply a discount where the patient only pays for the four most expensive items on a sliding scale. The business rules use the minimum allowed price in the official gazette to control the level of discount.

Invoice bundling

The client has complex cycle requirements for determining when to create invoices for different situations and how to group the charges on the invoices. These are configured into workflows which automatically generate invoices at the appropriate times.

Teaching hospitals

Complexities due to local variations in charging models were easily configured into PBRC's enterprise billing logic. For example, PBRC calculates charges and splits revenue differently for teaching hospitals where the university shares the cost of delivering services and receives a revenue share as payment for university doctors working at the hospital.

NEP Obstetric Services

The client requested a non-standard NEP Obstetrics module to manage the growing demand for obstetric services from mainland China by non-eligible persons (NEP). PHS delivered the functionality to handle registration, printing and issuing of certificates, as well as booking antenatal appointments, tracking attendance, and receipting payments. The flexibility of PBRC's configurable logic allows the client to maintain this module in compliance with future policy changes.

Increased business agility was demonstrated by a Radiology charging policy change. Shortly after the go-live, the client needed to change the radiology bundling logic, which had the most complicated business rules. PHS consultants worked with the client to rework the business rules and deployed this mid-production. The transition went smoothly, and the new charges took effect without impacting the previous charges or affecting the go-live schedules. This was an excellent demonstration of the system's business agility.

4.2 Innovation

In the case of health cost/revenue and billing management, there is a series of distinct transformations that are required to deliver value to the organization by managing the inherently complex many-to-many relationship between input raw cost factors and output revenue line items.

There are three major transformations required to resolve these many-to-many relationships:

- Transform unqualified raw data as supplied by external systems, into validated and standardized data that appropriately describes the required input costs;
- Transform validated, standardized input costs into the neutral idiom of the rules metaphor;
- Transform the costs now described by the idiom into the value-added outcomes required by each user of the application – new values, new reports, new workflows.

These three transformational phases form a standard design pattern for solutions that need to manage complex many-to-many rules matrices between inputs and outputs.

Firstly, raw data is input to the rules. Raw data describes the external reality. In most cases, the raw data is approximately equally available to all organizations because it is inherent to the domain – it is commodity-like, which allows the COTS application interfaces to be standardized. The rules that were involved in on-boarding this data into the domain of the rules are tactical in nature, essentially designed to ensure that the quality and quantity of data is sufficient enough to be able to achieve the ultimate purpose of the rules (e.g. billing values). These are the validation and acquisition rules.

Once the raw data has been acquired and validated, it starts its transformation journey towards the idiom of the organization that is seeking to harvest value from the data. It is normal for this intermediate step to generate a completely new state that is described in quite different terms to that of the raw data, but which is nonetheless internally consistent with it.

For instance, ward arrival and departure times for both patients and staff in the raw data might be transformed into an apportioned cost per hour per patient in the intermediate format, before the final transformation into actual billing items as defined by contracts, which might then include per diem payments, co-pays, lump sum payments etc. Note the distinct transformations – preparation and input of raw data into the idiom that is aligned with the purpose, then into the outputs, namely new state values, reports and workflows.

The three basic steps described above can be further complicated by internal domain and organizational variations.

It usually requires a range of subject matter expertise to validate and transform each of the domain-specific elements into the billing or costing idiom. Consequently, there is a rules topology that has multiple dimensions, starting with the basic three steps – validation, transformation into the idiom, derivation of outcomes.

This is then compounded by areas of domain expertise on the input side (see the 26 models of the client's billing repository below), and by the management disciplines that require the outcomes (billing, accounting, audit/compliance, operations/workflow, personnel management, etc.).

Decision Models ☐

- PayorDeterminationRules
- s10PPMI
- s12IPAdmissionFee
- s13IPMaintenanceFeePatient
- s14IPMaintenanceFeeAccompany
- s15IPDoctorFee
- s16InpatientDiet
- s21OPAttendenceFee
- s22FCSActualCharges
- s236AandE
- s2ActualCharges
- s31DayHospitalServices
- s32DayHospitalDiet
- s4CommunityServices
- s61PathologyServices
- s62RadiologyBundling
- s62RadiologyServices
- s63DiagnosticTherapeutic
- s64Operations
- s65Rehabilitation
- s71ObstetricPackage
- s81CertificateAndMedicalReports
- s82HearingAidsEarMoulds
- s83DentalTreatment
- s84MiscellaneousServices
- s9AdministrativeCharge

The above is a screenshot taken directly from the rules' development tool.

The rules topology might involve dozens of substantial algorithms (which we call decision models) that all need to be orchestrated in a single process to onboard the reality as described by the raw data and to ultimately produce the variety of outcomes that are desired by the various internal and external consumers.

In order to manage the navigation of various use cases through this topology, we have developed the concept of a control model. A control model is another algorithm whose purpose is to orchestrate the flow of each transactional use case (in this case, a patient encounter) through the topology.

The control model also allows us to add another dimension to the rules topology – that is time. Over time, we need to add and change the models that comprise the topology. If we run our use case from last year through the rules topography, it should obey the rules that applied last year. This requires an 'effective date' concept that is universal across commercial rules use cases. With a control model, we can orchestrate the application of complete decision models through time.

Providing each specialty with a unique decision model gives the business the ability to fine-tune hospital cost and revenue management without impacting other rules or the application itself. These changes can be made and deployed locally at any time. The conversion of unique cost structures into a standard idiom provides a value-added bridge, a 'safe-harbour' that allows the business to resolve the complex many-to-many relationship between input costs and revenue received, at the individual item level.

Dealing with the cost aggregation separately from the revenue item generation significantly reduces complexity – no one person or algorithm have to deal with the end-to-end complexity. In fact, the complexity 'emerges' from the integration of multiple simpler sets of rules, each of which is of manageable complexity by individual subject matter experts (SMEs) – dealing with the cost complexity alone and separate from the revenue complexity gives us complexity times two; trying to resolve the many-to many relationships in a single algorithm gives us complexity squared.

The major innovation is to reduce the complexity of the whole by addressing it via many individually simpler models and to then reassemble those models into an end-to-end solution on a just-in-time basis inside the rules engine, using a rules topology with a control decision model to orchestrate the multiple parts. The concept of a control model to orchestrate the topology is novel and reduces the complexity as it is seen by individual rules authors – no individual or group needs to see or address the full scope of complexity.

4.3 Impact and Implementation

The approach taken for this Project, and repeated throughout the PHS Initiative, is to allow the customer to use any preferred strategy for the internal management of their rules. An initial roadmap for the required rules topology is provided by PHS. It is the customer's responsibility to provide the rules within the constraints of the topology, regardless of whether they use default rules supplied by PHS, their own rules, or a combination thereof.

This approach allowed the project to quickly develop the original topology, which includes the 26 decision models in the preceding screenshot that cross 26 areas of expertise and are supported by 155 reference tables to provide a complete, correct, and consistent enterprise-wide set of rules.

The 26 decision models shown above generate ~300,000 lines of Java code when deployed, which demonstrates the scale of logic involved. This volume of code makes the rules a substantial component of the overall solution.

The complete set of rules was developed in approximately ten weeks of rules development effort, including seven weeks consultancy support from the rules vendor, within the nearly two-year development and implementation effort for the entire PBRC.

The rules have been fully supported by the client without vendor support since go-live ago.

This project demonstrated improved development and operational efficiency while addressing enterprise-wide complexity for a substantial organization.

5. HURDLES OVERCOME

Some specific hurdles itemized by the PBRC Project team include:
- Managing User and Regional Executive expectations – where there was a very high level of expectation that the new PBRC would deliver complete flexibility for the foreseeable future, satisfy all of the functional deficiencies inherent in the old home-grown application, and provide significant additional functionality to cater for requirements not previously covered by a software solution. Requests for functional enhancements were further driven by the knowledge that the software was under development when the implementation started, and the cultural change from implementing commercial off the shelf software (COTS) rather than an in-house developed application.
- Occasional significant variations in business practice and interpretation of Government policy and billing rules between management regions,

prompting the need to obtain consensus between regional management and users to define a common set of rules that were acceptable across all entities.

- Highly complex integration requirements arising from the number of feeder systems that needed to automatically provide essential data to the new PBRC to enable automation of the billing process, compounded by the need to retrofit a message-based integration architecture to existing client applications – 18 separate systems required 58 distinct interfaces. In addition, a significant number of data gaps in the essential data required from feeder systems needed to be closed by the integration solution, along with data mapping to resolve variations in service codes used by the various regions.

- To eliminate the need to have a very long transition from old to new systems with both running in parallel for a significant period of time, very large amounts of data needed to be migrated from the legacy to the new PBRC. The migration process was in itself a complex project as it was not a simple one-to-one transfer of data but involved a considerable amount of data enrichment on the way through.

- The Pilot site status of the implementation arising from the selection of a new generation software product that had not previously been implemented as an Enterprise-wide solution for such a large and complex organization. The testing strategy, therefore, needed to be very detailed and extremely thorough to ensure all potential business scenarios were covered as well as meeting demanding performance goals.

- Ongoing scope change caused by the addition of new functionality to solve previously out of scope business problems, and enhancement of current product functionality i.e. over the life of the implementation project, PBRC moved several years forward in a normal COTS software development lifecycle.

5.1 Management

Belief in the outcome is a key issue when developing at this scale because the elapsed development time becomes a critical factor in its own right.

The rules technology has its own on-board execution and testing environment so that rules can be developed and tested in parallel with the development of the underlying applications.

This provides 'quick wins' by making key business outcomes visible early in the process, helping to sustain belief and giving breathing room to the more traditional SDLC elements in the Project.

5.2 Business

A critical objective of the Project was to enable customer ownership and management of the rules. This was achieved by working closely with the SMEs, who were customer staff, to empower them in managing their own rules. Previously, these rules were codified in system code in multiple systems and were not visible or directly available to the SMEs.

In this Project, the transfer of active rule management was fully supported by the rules tool vendor, so that during the development of each and every set of rules, there was an active process to handover rules understanding and ownership. When each set of rules was finished, the new SME custodians assumed ownership going forward. As a result, handover was almost simultaneous with go-live.

5.3 Organization Adoption

Testing was a major issue for an enterprise system of this scale with nearly 1,000 active users at a dozen different locations.

The client developed some 14,000 test cases in preparation for meticulous and rigorous user acceptance testing. These test cases were developed by the client implementation team in consultation with users. Over the course of the user acceptance testing process, the project team invited selected users to the head office for week-long sessions to test the scripted scenarios and to undertake freehand testing.

During the implementation process, the client implementation team logged some 2,000 support logs covering functional, as well as performance issues. Majority of the issues were resolved and closed prior to the first Go-live, with a few deferred for incorporation as subsequent enhancements to the core software.

Some of the logged issues related to requirements that had never been delivered before by a COTS billing package and resulted in the addition of new functionality into the core product in order to deliver a robust and fit for purpose solution.

For example, social services can issue waiver certificates which apply discounts to charges in a logical but complex fashion. Where a patient has multiple certificates with overlapping periods, there is a set priority which is used to determine which certificate gets applied to the charges. But there are other receipting systems upstream of PBRC, and a patient may have presented to them a different waiver certificate. It is important that PBRC retains the integrity of the receipting which occurs upstream. New functionality was therefore added to enable exceptions to the waiver priority, with specific charges being reserved, so as to allow waiving by one specific waiver certificate and no other. By necessity, this has been designed to work even if the certificate and the charge have not yet been created in PBRC. There were many such significant enhancements to the core system.

Go-Live

The first phase was rolled out to 318 users in seven participating hospitals.

Radiology format change

Two months prior to the go-live, there was a change in the Radiology message format. This had a major impact on the automated interface linking the Radiology system to PBRC. The interface was modified and deployed within a month, without affecting the go-live deadline.

Rehearsals

The first go-live underwent three cut-over rehearsals, where selected participating users used the new system for one week, concentrating on one thing at a time:
- The 1st rehearsal focused on product readiness
- The 2nd focused on staff and hospital readiness
- The 3rd focused on readiness for handling the transaction volumes.

Go-Live Sequence

On day one of the Go-live process, the old system for the relevant hospitals was switched off, and the new system switched on.

Billing operations continued by using manual processing for one week, while data from the legacy system for each separate go-live site was migrated into the new enterprise system.

At the start of the next week, all billing and receipting activities commenced using the new system.

Performance

The go-live went smoothly with most attention being focused on data volumes and performance tuning. Application issues that showed up were minor edge cases and workarounds were used while the issues were being resolved.

Radiology charging policy change

Shortly after this go-live, the client needed to change the radiology bundling logic, which had the most complicated business rules. PHS consultants worked with the client to rework the business rules and deployed this mid production. The transition went smooth and the new charges took effect without impacting the previous charges or affecting the go-live schedules. This was an excellent demonstration of system's business agility.

Remaining Users

All other users were converted in two tranches on schedule and without incident.

6. BENEFITS

6.1 Cost Savings / Time Reductions

PBRC design philosophy separates business logic and high-level workflow processing logic from the core software processing functions, to allow for customization by configuration rather than changing core software program code. This met the client's top priority of business agility.

Business logic

PBRC uses a rules engine which has a graphical interface for modelling business rules. Client staff can modify these rules in response to changes in business policies and government regulations and deploy these changes swiftly. For example:

- "Income splitting" rules to calculate the division of revenue between public and private practitioners, based on individual agreements.
- "Radiology bundling" rules to generate individual charges for all services, calculate several possible packaged permutations and select the cheapest package and individual charges for the patient.

Processing logic

PBRC uses a workflow engine for controlling billing processing. client staff can configure the workflows to customize the billing processes. For example:

- Eligibility checking — perform web service callouts to the public sector (for employee rates) and the immigration department (for citizen rates) to verify financial class.
- Administration fees – where an additional charge (late payment fee) is automatically created once a patient's invoice becomes overdue.

Consolidated invoices

PBRC servers are located at the client's data centers, serving users in hospitals and clinics. PBRC bills for services from all locations in a consolidated patient invoice, thus simplifying invoicing and payment for both patients and HKHA, resulting in a reduced number of transactions and improved efficiency.

Reduced labor costs

Increased automation reduces the amount of manual input and labor cost, as fewer clerks are needed to perform manual procedures.

Reduced operational costs

By consolidating previously separate systems into one new enterprise billing system, the client experienced cost savings (e.g. computer servers, office space).

Reduced maintenance & support effort

With a centralized system, the client's IT can more easily resource maintenance and support. For example, upgrades are now performed once instead of multiple times as is required by a distributed architecture. System administrators find it much easier to monitor and tune one system instead of many. Additionally, the clients' PCs require minimal maintenance and support with PBRC launching from a web browser, where relevant software upgrades are performed automatically.

6.2 Increased Revenues

Invoicing and receipting at Point-of-Service

In some circumstances, the client's policy requires payment prior to treatment with the generation of invoices on patient arrival at the point-of-service. This time-sensitivity places significant performance demands on billing processing speed, especially at peak times. PBRC's scalable architecture allows real-time addition of software agents and hardware servers to meet fluctuations in processing demand.

Monthly statements:

Patients with outstanding accounts are sent itemized monthly statements, with amounts paid & owed and an optional reminder of when payment is due. This makes it easier for patients to settle their accounts and results in improved cash flow and reduced outstanding debts.

6.3 Quality Improvements

Reliability

With their complicated business logic configured into the system, the client can be confident that charges are being applied correctly, consistently and reliably. Discrepancies due to human error are eliminated by this automation.

Centralized revenue collection

With the new enterprise-wide system, invoices can now be paid at any of the client's facilities regardless of where treatment is received.

Standardized procedures

The patient-based system has centralized billing services and introduced consistency to the client's billing as all hospitals are now using the same system and procedures.

Enterprise reporting

With a single enterprise-wide repository, prompt and accurate reporting across hospitals, patients, and services is now possible.

Organizational management

PBRC supports central administration by the client's head office and distributed management by the client's regions.

Corporate branding

All PBRC documents such as invoices and statements are custom formatted, and the client's IT staff can easily deploy changes by simply updating the document templates.

Efficient revenue collection across all locations

Previously, payments could only be collected by hospitals and clinics for services provided at that location. PBRC now detects outstanding amounts for all locations and the client can therefore request payment for outstanding amounts when a patient presents for treatment at any location.

7. BEST PRACTICES, LEARNING POINTS AND PITFALLS

7.1 Best Practices and Learning Points

✓ *Developing a rules topography to guide rules development is an important precursor step to take in any rules development and is essential for effective normalization of rules.*

✓ *Rules should be fully normalized – this means the fewest number of rules to implement the required algorithms, means that the algorithm is in its simplest form.*

✓ *Normalized rules allow greater agility (less to change), fewer errors, more reuse, and less development effort.*

✓ *When rules are normalized, it follows that patterns for reuse of rules must be achieved at many levels, with special emphasis on the decision model itself. This is the driver for a rules topology.*

✓ *Identify and develop the core rules first. These are the rules that define the* **purpose of the system**. *Then follow through with development of transformation rules, validation rules, and finally workflow and reporting rules. That is, build from the inside out, starting with the core, and working back to the inputs (via transformations and validations), and then working forward to the outputs (new state values, reports, workflows).*

✓ *Use the best subject matter experts to develop the reusable rules in order to codify and then leverage their expertise.*

7.2 Pitfalls

✗ *In general, avoid the antithesis of the above.*

✗ *Don't build monolithic rules structures that mix purpose and expertise.*

✗ *Don't mix rules by type in the same algorithm (e.g. core calculation, transformation, validation, workflow, etc.).*

8. COMPETITIVE ADVANTAGES

PHS takes on what no other organization seeks to do. For example, with PBRC, PHS recognized that public hospital billing was fragmented and inefficient and no vendor actually specialized in patient billing. Existing systems were all linked to a clinical application, albeit large multinationals, but if you wanted a Pharmacy, Radiology or Pathology system, then you bought that system, and each came with their own billing module. This implied separate staff, training, accounts receivables, etc., for each system. It also meant that at times, the decision on what clinical system to buy was greatly influenced by the appropriateness of the billing module that came with it.

What PHS has done is to say, 'don't worry about the billing module that comes with any clinical application. PHS has developed a fit-for-purpose enterprise-wide billing application that integrates to all clinical systems and is dedicated to automating and simplifying the billing process across all customer clinical application'.

What's more, billing rules were typically coded into the application but because a billing system is in essence an accounting package, while billing rules change all the time, it was disastrous to have a system that should remain consistent in its behavior while the code was changing all the time. PHS realized very early on in the development of PBRC that an appropriate logic/rules engine would be ideal to code billing rules. This decision was made in 2004, fully 18 months before Gartner published an article extolling the benefits of adopting a rules engine as part of any software development project.

PHS has a four-step commercial strategy to encourage customers to stay committed to the substantial advantages described above:

- PHS doesn't license as a SaaS model. We license with an upfront license fee and implementation and then a 20% annual support fee. The sale is harder to get but this ensures that as new tech is introduced, which is cheaper and would likely undercut an existing SaaS model pricing, that new price will still be much higher than what our clients are paying for at 20%.
- Maintain a very high Net Promoter Score (hovers between 65 and 75. (Apple has a 70) by providing great support to all our clients
- Invest significantly in R&D to keep the product continually fresh and relevant.
- Following the initial 3- to 5-year Term, offer our clients new modules (developed under R&D) free of charge with a three-year renewal.

Given clients are satisfied, have access to new functionality every three years, free of charge and would have to pay more for an alternative solution, PHS is able to keep clients long-term. In 16 years, only one client has ever stopped using a PHS system. That is how PHS sustains completive advantage.

9. TECHNOLOGY

The use of a rules product fosters a fundamental redesign of the traditional SDLC by fully separating the development and automation of business policy (deciding) from the development of the system's activities that support it (doing). This is effective in spawning a 'Business Policy Development Life Cycle' that is managed independently of and alongside the traditional System Development Life Cycle. The rules technology used offers a number of compelling features to support this

Scale and Complexity: The rules development paradigm, and its supporting decision engine was required to deal with substantial complexity across the entire scope of the enterprise. That is, the scope of rules, and their interrelationships, extended across all aspects of the enterprise. With 42 hospitals and 121 clinics supporting 20 million patient encounters per year in our reference Project, the scale was substantial. In this case, the rules technology was able to address many distinct subdomains (e.g. each specialist area) in a clear, consistent, and coordinated manner without introducing additional complexity.

Performance: Millions of items per day are being processed, with outcomes required in real-time at the point of discharge for the patient, and sometimes before. The rules technology generates compiled code that can run 'in-process', so that minimal processing overhead is incurred. Rules processing per output item is in the single millisecond range and it means that the overall application is able to achieve the customer's desired performance benchmarks. The rules process is stateless and thread-safe, so as many instances of the rules can be used as required to achieve unlimited throughput while maintaining fast response times.

Ease of Use: The initial rules approach and rules development was performed by PHS with the assistance of the rules vendor. Seven weeks of assistance from the rules vendor delivered approximately 70% of the rules development, with the balance delivered by PHS and the client's domain experts. Rules training for the client occurred as an intended by-product of the rules development process, so that after a few days additional training, the rules were handed over to the customer as part of the go-live transition. This specific customer has managed the rules independently (a period of seven years) without a single service call to the rules vendor.

Versatility: In addition to the 'business end' of business rules (calculations, et al.), the rules can be used for more traditional IT functions that also rely on standard, user-defined logic including validation and transformation (the heart of EVTL) at the entry point; and reporting and workflow (what do we need to do now) at the exit point. This demonstrates versatility in how the rules can be used.

Data Agility: A simple change to an XML schema is all that is required to introduce new facts into the scope of the rules by the application. Data can be added at will on an ongoing basis and are immediately available to subsequent rules processing.

Time Sensitive: All rules are effective dated at every level and are always executable as at any effective date – past, present, or future. This means that long-lived use cases can span changes in business policy and always be evaluated according to the applicable policy at the time, which is itself a policy issue to be controlled by rules (do you charge as at the time of admission, time of discharge, re-price on annual boundaries, etc.).

Version Consistency: The technical format of the rules has been backwards compatible since the inception of the product (2001), so that version upgrades in the rules are never mandated by technology requirements. Of course, new product features can only be accessed with new versions. However, the rules themselves will always execute without a change in all future versions of the rules product.

On Board Execution: The rules tool has an onboard execution engine and extensive support for both on-board step-by-step and full regression/simulation testing. This allows an independent rules development cycle that can start early in the project to provide morale-boosting optics and important requirements feedback for the more traditional SDLC developments, as well as significantly speeding up development and reducing testing overheads across the project. The complete independence of the rules development cycle provides many advantages, including multi-party rules development; rules production prior to, during, and after applications development; and smaller and more durable applications.

As a consequence, PHS achieves the following key Value Propositions:
- 100% alignment of systems-based decision making with business policy, because the business owners have hands-on custody and control of the policy definitions being used by the system.
- Increased agility with reduced business risk through business modeling and empirical testing of policy definitions prior to automated generation and implementation.
- Significant reduction in the business cost of developing and implementing automated business policy.
- Further reduction in software development cost, time, & risk through reduced system complexity, fewer moving parts, and clear separation of concerns.

10. THE TECHNOLOGY AND SERVICE PROVIDERS

PowerHealth Solutions (Australia) powerhealthsolutions.com

PowerHealth Solutions is an international healthcare software company specializing in Costing & Revenue, Enterprise Billing and Safety & Quality software for hospitals and other healthcare organizations.

PowerHealth Solutions supplies the PowerBilling and Revenue Collection™ and PowerPerformance Manager™ applications.

IDIOM Limited (New Zealand) www.idiomsoftware.com

IDIOM Limited supplies the IDIOM Decision Manager™, which was used to construct all decision models referenced in this case study. IDIOM Decision Manager™ is a graphical modelling tool that is used by subject matter experts to build, test, and deploy very large and complex decision models for any domain.

Rabobank, the Netherlands
Nominated by Oracle, the Netherlands

1. Executive Summary / Abstract

Having a business rules solution enabled Rabobank to get a major concern, Customer Due Diligence, under control, in a relative short period of time. The benefits are huge and versatile: real-time & batch wise checking, performing over millions of records, traceability of decisions, auditability, consistency in logic, flexibility in business logic changes and last, but not least, predictability of impact of rule changes.

2. Overview

Multiple checklists, techniques and systems have been used in the support of Customer Due Diligence for several years by multiple local banks and departments. This led to an increasing backlog of customer reviews. In order to get control and less-involved parties, Rabobank decided to centralize the required business logic with a rule engine which can be used in different processes.

The rule engine was chosen as the preferred technology over a data quality tool and a marketing tool, due to high reliability, mature management organization, suitable for complex business rules, flexibility and readable rules in natural language.

The realized benefits are indeed: uniformity, consistency; continuous monitoring; transparency, flexibility and forecasting.

Moving from local distributed processes to a centralized one with a single source of automated decisions was a challenge. Other encountered challenges were finding a balance between risk control and practical operation, automation and employee involvement, simplifying and employee consciousness. From a technical perspective, large sets of hierarchical data structures and creating a rule base with a complex unreadable erroneous risk model in Excel as starting point has been a challenge.

3. Business Context

Rabobank is an international financial services provider operating on the basis of cooperative principles. As a cooperative bank, Rabobank is a socially-responsible bank. It serves approximately 8.7 million clients around the world and is one of the largest cooperatives in the Netherlands with nearly two million members. Members are more than just customers, they have a voice in deciding the bank's strategic course. Rabobank is committed to making a substantial contribution towards achieving wealth and prosperity in the Netherlands and to resolving the food issue worldwide.

Early 2017, Rabobank became one bank. The more than hundred local banks ceased to be legal entities by themselves with their own banking license and started operating under one banking license as one cooperative bank. The local Rabobanks form the most finely-meshed banking network in the Netherlands.

Just like for every bank, Customer Due Diligence is a major concern for the Rabobank. The bank is obliged to comply with the Money Laundering and Financing Terrorism Act (from the Dutch 'Wet Witwassen en Financiering Terrorisme', in short WWFT). This means that every customer must be checked against the WWFT.

Each Dutch bank is continuously checked by the Dutch National Bank (de Nederlandse Bank, DNB) to verify if they are compliant to the WWFT. Non-compliancy, e.g. not knowing all the customers, missing processes, malfunctioning maintenance or accepting malicious customers will result in warnings, reputation damage or even very high fines.

It is a serious task for Rabobank having to make sure that not only are its millions of customers checked against the WWFT but also that none slips through. Customer Due Diligence is about risk containment on a large scale.

When the WWFT became effective in July 2008, customers were initially divided in risk categories by SQL queries based on data initially collected and intended for marketing purposes. Some customers needed to be reviewed on a regular basis depending on their risk category to establish the bank's risk and to have control measures. The review was a manual, paper-based process. Each branch of the bank did the review to the best of their knowledge and ability.

In 2010, monitoring was implemented, again based on SQL queries on marketing data, to verify if the customer data was correct and complete for the WWFT. An indicator on customer level was introduced in 2012 in the CRM system to prevent sales when risks were identified for that customer by a coded business service.

The first steps to model-based working were taken when automated support of the manual paper-based process was introduced in 2013 for the employees in the CRM system. The first to start using a minimal set of business rules for customer validation and acceptance was the STP customer onboarding online process of one-man businesses in 2015.

The first complete risk model was translated into a rule base in 2016. The model enhanced the customers risk category with several risk indicators. The automated review process was extended with a web-interview of the risk model in the rule base. With the given answers and hardly any customer data, the rule base also calculates the level of risk per risk indicator.

A further refinement of risk assessment was made in 2017 when the rule base started to reassess the risk after user input on the calculated risk. When receiving clear instruction of the executive of the WWFT a manual investigation was started with queries on the customers which weren't regularly reviewed.

Now that the architecture with the rule engine and a risk model in the rule base is in place an acceleration of functionality is possible in 2018. Recently, the query-based monitoring of customer data and investigations of not being reviewed customers were replaced by batch-wise business rule execution resulting in:

- Monitoring of all customers to check if customer data is WWFT compliant and informing employees when action is needed.
- Assessing the risks of all customers who never have been reviewed.
- Automated risk reassessment of all reviewed customers with changed data.
- The possibility to determine the impact of new rules or rule changes on all the customers and the organisation.

The rules and customer data used in batch are also used in the web-interview in the real time review process, to further help the employee by either giving or suggesting answers.

Further development will be using external data in the risk assessment and moving from generic control-based monitoring and regularly reviewing many to precise event driven, only-when-needed reviewing.

4. THE KEY INNOVATIONS

4.1 Business and Operational Impact

Establishment or improvement of compliance capabilities or traceability:

The compliance capabilities have been improved firstly by replacing a manual paper-based review process with a dynamic rule-based web-interview checking risks more precise with a higher granularity.

Secondly by replacing the query-based monitoring with a rule base for batch-wise risk and data checking. This changed the scale from only regularly reviewing some medium and high-risk customers to checking all customers regularly if reviews are needed.

On the last audit, the auditors were able to ultimately trace back to the implemented business rules. Because the executable rules are set in natural language, we were able to answer and validate their questions on by reviewing the rules without the need for runtime testing.

Traceability is guaranteed by storing the rule base version with each risk check/review and by traceability links in rules to the Customer Due Diligence standards.

Proven importance of getting Customer Due Diligence under control:

Implementing the business rules solution with an automated process in the CRM system eliminated the previously increasing backlog of customer reviews.

The last internal audit did not find errors nor missing checks.

Customers cannot make purchases without a risk detection check. The use of business rules ensures fast and reliable risk classifications which can be incrementally automated increasing the set of customers that can be serviced without manual actions.

Reviewing more millions of customers is too time-consuming, too expensive and unfavorable for the customer. Using business rules make it possible to know all our customers on a weekly basis or getting to know them directly when they are new.

We have proven to implement rule changes within the two days of the SLA which effects all channels and all customers.

Enhanced consistency of business outcomes, decisions, or customer experience:

When the risk classifications were based on employee knowledge of the legislation there were regularly inconsistencies and subsequently slowdowns of the customer onboarding process. The business rules solution eliminated those problems. It brought a uniform way of working and consistent application of the rules.

Instead of tedious forms, employees are now guided through all the inquiries and only asked questions when needed.

Improved understandability, accessibility, or reusability of business rules or decisions:

The initial limited number of rules implemented in SQL queries and a coded business service were hard to validate and maintain consistently. Reusability was out of the question.

With the centrally defined, declarative, natural language rules, it has not only become easy to maintain complex risk classification and calculation rules but also understandable for the business. Business reviews are done directly on the rule base. Reusability is achieved, e.g. both batch and on-demand use the same ruleset.

Substantial size, scope or quality of governance process or rule / decision management:

Next to a central rule base was also the governance of Customer Due Diligence which was organized centrally with a new central department for policy creation and reviewing the more risk full customers.

Having a rule base has helped to remove inconsistencies and errors in the devised policy.

Technically, also the data was centralized by having a data mart with the sole purpose of compliancy removing the dependency with marketing.

Better data quality or metrics:

Customer data is monitored to check if it is WWFT compliant. Employees are informed when actions are needed such as actions to register an UBO, legal representative or determine the risk category.

Although the purpose of the business rules solution for risk identification is not to solve data quality issues, it validates the incoming data to check whether a valid classification can be made based on that data. When this check fails, no interview can be conducted, and the employee needs to correct the customer data first. This process enforces data integrity constraints across the organization.

Improved customer service, customer retention, or quality improvements:

The customer onboarding process has sped up due to an automated consistent rule-based web-interview.

Quality has improved because risk detection is done consistently across all channels and employees of local banks.

4.2 Innovation

- From non-transparent and erroneous Excel formulas to explicit natural language rules with logical verification.
- Single point of definition of the risk model used in all channels: local banks, online applications and batch processes.
- Independency from the CRM-system release cycle, speeding up delivery significantly.
- Changes in policy regarding industry risks or country risks can be deployed within two days.
- Context driven rules enable customization per channel or mode of operation.
- Interviews are enhanced with context dependent instructions helping employees in complex matters, improving quality and speeding up processes.
- New data streams can be added incrementally without major architectural changes.
- Last, but not least, by reassessing customers with prior stored risk detection checks using updated customer data, changes in risk can be detected.
- Changes in risk classification are either caused by changed customer data or by changed policies. In this manner, all customers are continuously being monitored.

When enough data has been integrated in the model, it will be possible to migrate to completely event-driven compliancy instead of periodical risk assessments.

On top of that, when only stored checks are used without updated customer data, it is possible to evaluate the impact of just the policy changes.

The table below shows the results of the latest Customer Due Diligence Change in Circumstances batch. The table has been filtered for customers that have a current risk classification at medium or high-risk that is higher than both the prior and the accepted risk classification. The increase in the number of high- or medium-risk customers can be used to calculate the workload of follow-up investigations.

Results CDD CiC Batch

Risk difference analysis of customers with a prior risk detection check record
based on current customer data and prior interview answers

Execution date	12-7-2018	*Legenda*
Environment	PROD	1.Low	Low risk
Number of assessed customers	100%	2.Medium	Medium risk
Riskmodel version	11,1	3.High	High risk
Rulebase version	196	0.No outcome	Data integrity issue
Deployment version	87		

Customer type	Accepted risk	Prior calculated risk	Current calculated risk	Percentage	Current risk > Accepted risk	Current risk > Prior risk
Person	1.Low	1.Low	2.Medium	1,6315%	TRUE	TRUE
Person	1.Low	1.Low	3.High	0,0330%	TRUE	TRUE
Person	1.Low	2.Medium	3.High	0,0671%	TRUE	TRUE
Person	1.Low	0.No outcome	2.Medium	0,0169%	TRUE	TRUE
Person	1.Low	0.No outcome	3.High	0,0021%	TRUE	TRUE
Person	2.Medium	1.Low	3.High	0,0070%	TRUE	TRUE
Person	2.Medium	2.Medium	3.High	0,0170%	TRUE	TRUE
Person	2.Medium	0.No outcome	3.High	0,0012%	TRUE	TRUE
Person	0.Risk unknown	1.Low	2.Medium	0,0007%	TRUE	TRUE
Person	0.Risk unknown	2.Medium	3.High	0,0004%	TRUE	TRUE
Organisation	1.Low	1.Low	2.Medium	0,1587%	TRUE	TRUE
Organisation	1.Low	2.Medium	3.High	0,0007%	TRUE	TRUE
Organisation	1.Low	0.No outcome	2.Medium	0,0004%	TRUE	TRUE
Organisation	2.Medium	2.Medium	3.High	0,0007%	TRUE	TRUE
		Total		1,9374%		

Statistics june for high/medium risk customers	Nr of sessions	%high and medium	Total time followup investigations in man days
Basic interviews	20000		
Current nr of followup investigations	2167	**10,8342%**	203,1
Increase nr of followup investigations	387	**1,9374%**	36,3
Total estimated nr of followup investigations	2554	**12,7716%**	239,5

4.3 Impact and Implementation

Successful initiative to capture and express business rules, decision tables, terminology and concept models

The Customer Due Diligence policy used to be described in more than hundred different documents. Before 2017, the 102 local banks, being legal entities by themselves, each had their own paper checklist version of the Customer Due Diligence policy.

A part of the scattered policy was reduced by one risk model in Excel. Processes were uniformed to an automated one in the CRM system. The risk model in Excel was replaced by a rule-based web-interview in the automated process in the CRM system.

Other parts of the scattered policy were implemented in a batch-wise rule base for continuous monitoring.

Significant scope and scale of the initiative's implementation

The business rules solution had impact on all the local banks and the thousands of customer-facing employees. A new separate department, dealing with the more complex cases was established, now consisting of 400 employees. Not only regularly reviewing some medium and high-risk customers but checking all, more than ten million customers regularly, if reviews are needed.

Successful implementation of advanced business rules or decision concepts

New rules were introduced for more in-depth risk control or supporting the employee with awareness messages or prefilled answers based on customer data. Their impact can be forecasted by running what-if scenarios

5. HURDLES OVERCOME

5.1 Management

From a management perspective, the biggest hurdle was moving from local distributed processes to a centralized process and a single source of automated decisions.

5.2 Business

CAMS is the unit responsible for the risk model and keeping it in sync with the effective legislation. People working on the risk model, always have potential customer risks in mind, tend to be 'risk-oriented' and not afraid to describe and model every possible risk they can think of. As this would potentially result in a huge workload, the more operationally oriented people will vote against such policies. These discussions are still going on, but eventually a consensus has been reached and, additionally, discussions are supported by better metrics.

5.3 Organization Adoption

Risk assessment has not been fully automated. Part of the basic review is completely automated, and part must be completed by an employee. The basic review will then generate the follow-up questions that need to be asked in the follow-up investigation. Answering these follow-up questions is not an automated process, except for the possibility to enter the answers in a web form and automated workload management. Not all employees can adequately perform a follow-up investigation, so Rabobank is still struggling with the routing of each assessment. Routing rules are continuously being tuned in order to send each assessment to the correct unit.

Another side to automating risk assessments is the tendency of employees to stop thinking and just click through the interview as fast as possible. This may result in lower risk classifications than is appropriate. One of the main features currently being developed is enriching the interview with awareness messages and showing the answer to questions that has been given in the prior assessment.

5.4 Technology

5.4.1 Risk model implementation

The risk model was defined in an Excel, which hid the actual business and calculation rules through lots of references and lookup formulas in multiple sheets.

The enormous complexity that followed was unmaintainable and unreadable. In the migration to a rule-based solution, the only way to ensure the rules were correct was to literally reengineer the model by including a separate rule for each reference and formula.

That way, it was possible to use the Excel sheet to generate test-cases that could be tested on the rules, ensuring a correct model.

By having the rules explicit and readable like the following example, it immediately became clear where the model was at fault, inconsistent or redundant.

the score of question NPCDD08D01	
0	the answer of question NPCDD08D01 = "No" or the answer of question NPCDD08D01 = "Yes, xxxxx" or the answer of question NPCDD08D01 = "Yes, parent" or the answer of question NPCDD08D01 = "Yes, xxxxx" or the answer of question NPCDD08D01 = "Yes, xxxxx"
50	the answer of question NPCDD08D01 = "Yes, heir" or the answer of question NPCDD08D01 = "Yes, xxxxx"
100	the answer of question NPCDD08D01 = "Yes, xxxxx" or the answer of question NPCDD08D01 = "Yes, xxxxx" or the answer of question NPCDD08D01 = "Yes, xxxxx" or the answer of question NPCDD08D01 = "Yes, xxxxx" or the answer of question NPCDD08D01 = "Yes, trustee" or the answer of question NPCDD08D01 = "Yes, xxxxx" or the answer of question NPCDD08D01 = "Yes, xxxxx"
uncertain	other

Because of the large numbers of customers, the use of different versions of the Excel model and its opaque format, these inconsistencies had remained hidden.

The disadvantage of reengineering was that the unnecessary complexities in the Excel model were initially copied to the new rule solution. Only after the reengineering was finished that it became possible to remove them.

5.4.2 Data complexity

Validating customer compliancy involves checking the relations of the customer with other customers. Organizations or persons like curators, administrators, budget managers et al, may have hundreds, even thousands of related customers and parties. Organizations can be nested in a large organizational structure of many organizations that each may have a lot of related persons or other organizations. Some organizational structures exist form a graph with over 20,000 nodes.

To assess such large networked customers ideally, the whole graph is included in the case, but this led to performance issues, such as batches running over 37 hours. As solution, some of the rules were to be executed in the database to filter the huge trees. Filtering was done by including 'where-clauses' in the SQL queries that generate the views in the batch Database.

In order to still have single point of definition and be complete in the rules, the SQL-clauses are generated in the Excel rule tables. For instance, relevant for validating organizations are the countries of residence of Ultimate Beneficiary Owners (UBO's). To find the UBO's of an organization, all parents of the organization have to be traversed to check each related person to see whether that person is an UBO and where that person lives. Only a small number of relationship types are relevant to this search, so the search tree is pruned by selecting only those organizations and persons that are related with a relevant relationship type.

Checking the relevant relationship type is included in the rules, so it was possible to generate the 'where-clauses' by adding Excel string formulas to the rule tables themselves. Now, when relationship types are changed or added, the clauses change too and only must be copied to the SQL to reflect the new situation.

6. BENEFITS

6.1 Cost Savings, Time Reductions, Increased Revenues

The first and major concern of the Rabobank has been getting Customer Due Diligence under control. Consequently, efficiency has not been the main or even the second business driver. The number one business driver is being compliant to the WWFT: quality and auditability, being able to transparently and uniformly classify the millions of customers and parties and taking adequate measures for high- and medium-risk customers.

Because efficiency was and is not in focus and Customer Due Diligence related work has been a stream of activities going back to 2008, it is nearly impossible to establish a proper baseline. However, what is evident, is that the situation has drastically changed. The main benefits of the solution that is currently in place compared to the prior situation:

Uniform model application

In the prior situation, the Customer Due Diligence-policies used to be distributed over more than hundred documents that employees had to research to be able to apply the correct policies for each customer. The local banks used to create their own checklists and decision trees to do so. This resulted in very diverse and inconsistent ways of risk assessment. Traceability was virtually impossible.

In the current situation, customers are classified using a central risk model that is applied uniformly over all channels and customer processes.

Continuous monitoring

Not only customers are classified in a repeatable and uniform way, but also are continuously monitored by reassessing them on a weekly basis. In the future, when the business drivers will lean more toward efficiency, this will enable the Rabobank to decrease the number of assessments needed: currently, periodic reviews are a legal requirement, but when Rabobank can show to be in control by having event-driven Customer Due Diligence-checks, the necessary resources can be reduced significantly. Currently, at least 400 people in the Customer Due Diligence service centre and thousands at the local banks are performing risk assessments.

Transparency

Each decision regarding a customer can be traced back to the rules that supported it and, additionally, those rules can be linked to the relevant part of the effective policies.

Speed of change

New policies can be effectively and uniformly deployed in a matter of days. Changes in sanction-policies for countries that come into effect based on UN-directives must be implemented within two business days.

Such a high priority change now is matter of changing the country rule table, performing a regression test on the new version and deploying it to the hub.

Forecasting

New policies that are still being discussed can be applied in a what-if scenario to analyze the impact the policy will have. Since there has always been tension between risk oriented and operationally oriented business people, there is always discussion about new policies. Having the forecasting in place, these discussions can be fed with actual numbers.

6.3 Quality Improvements

The following quality improvements have been realized:

- The risk model is expressed in explicit, readable, natural language rules. This enables business validation of the model and easy expression of new requirements (there is no need any more to add complex formulas in Excel)
- Another advantage of the rule representation is that it is easily adaptable
- Separation of the business logic from the workflows and the CRM-system has enabled fast deployment of new policies.
- Having all rules in one place facilitates testing in one place. A large regression test set keeps the model consistent with every change.
- Operational statistics can be compared across all local banks
- Because all inferences and risk classifications are available during a risk assessment, the employee can be provided with context aware help items and alerts.
- The report that accompanies a stored risk detection check contains the same elements as generated by the rule engine.

7. BEST PRACTICES, LEARNING POINTS AND PITFALLS

7.1 Best Practices and Learning Points

- ✓ Have a dedicated delivery agile team for rule management as it is separate expertise.
- ✓ The whole team must conform to the guidelines/rule authoring directives.
- ✓ Business departments and other IT teams need to acknowledge when to use rules as the solution.
- ✓ Have business reviews directly on the rules resulting in good business involvement and flexibility.
- ✓ All disciplines should be available during review: subject matter expert, business process owner, rule author, ops engineer, architect.
- ✓ Reuse, single point of definition is a form of centralization: all stakeholders need to be aligned to be able to cope with changes.
- ✓ The architecture, data model and rulesets, need to granular and modular enough to be flexible in case of changes.
- ✓ Architecture of a rule base is a continuous balance of stability and change.
- ✓ Principles are good, but not set in stone. Working solutions are a balance between simplicity, complexity, adaptability, consistency and performance.
- ✓ Rules on large sets of hierarchical data structures are best done outside the rule base.

7.2 Pitfalls

- ✗ Requirements are written with workflow or procedure in mind.
- ✗ Rules are the new kid on the block: collaboration is lacking when the environment is not involved early, delaying integration. With production issues, the rule solution is the scapegoat.
- ✗ The rule authoring tool is very flexible in attribute formulation. Guidelines and directives are necessary to constrain the possibilities and keep things clean and maintainable.

8. COMPETITIVE ADVANTAGES

The ability to forecast impact of policy changes and to monitor all customers on a weekly basis is new in the banking market. The Dutch National Bank is more positive in the audits to Rabobank compared to competitors.

9. TECHNOLOGY

9.1 Infrastructure

Compliance at the Rabobank comprises several separate controlling applications: not only risk detection but also tax-reporting according to the Common Reporting Standard and its U.S. counterpart FATCA and client integrity as well.

These applications all use the same infrastructure, consisting of a CRM system that handles back-end processes, a data warehouse that stores all customer data and a business rules management and execution system that adds decisions to customer processes and data.

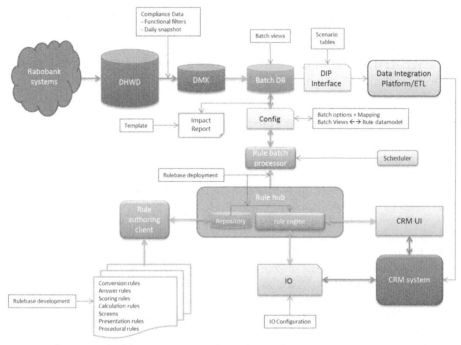

KCM Components Technical Architecture

In a normal scenario, for instance, onboarding of a new customer would start in the online app of the bank. When the first necessary data is collected and registered in the CRM system, a 'check'-module will determine which compliance checks apply to the customer under investigation.

A risk detection check is always necessary, so an activity is added to the queue that will trigger an employee of either a local bank or the Service Center Customer Due Diligence to conduct an interview in the form of a wizard embedded in the CRM system (CRM UI).

The questions, screens and calculated results are generated by the rule engine. The input data needed for the rule engine to start the interview and perform the calculations are retrieved from the CRM system through a SOAP API.

The interview can be stopped and resumed at will; the rule engine will resume the interview on the last screen visited.

The results of the interview are finally stored in the CRM system and exported to the data warehouse, on a daily basis.

From the data in the data warehouse, all data relevant to compliance is exported to a smaller dedicated data mart. From there on, the data is converted to a format that can be used by the batch processor

9.2 Batch process modes

The batch process, using the same underlying rule base, will retrieve each case in turn and output new risk classifications depending on the mode in which the batch is run. Three modes are distinguished:

9.2.1 Regression test/What-if

This mode is run on an ad-hoc basis when new changes are about to be deployed. In this mode, only the stored answers, including answers that were based on stored customer data, are used, resulting in risk classifications that are identical to the stored classifications when the same rules are applied.

When new or changed rules are applied, based on changed policy, then also a difference in outcomes is expected. For instance, if the percentage of high-risk customers goes up by two percent, then also the number of follow-up assessments increases by two percent.

Furthermore, when these changed rules are applied in the actual production batch, a number of extra activities are triggered resulting in more basic and follow-up assessments. Basic and follow-up assessments take 15 and 40 minutes on average, respectively.

The below table shows a fictional and simplified table of old and new results and the resulting change.

Customers policy April	Customers policy May	Difference
Low	Low	0
Low	Low	0
Medium	High	1
Low	Medium	1
Low	Low	0
High	High	0
Low	Low	0
Medium	Low	-1
Low	Low	0
Low	Medium	1
Low	Low	0
Low	Low	0
High	High	1
Low	Low	0
Low	Medium	1
Low	Low	0
Low	Low	0
Low	Low	0
Low	High	2
Medium	High	1
Low	Low	0
Low	Medium	1
Low	Low	0
Low	Low	0
	25	8
	Total change	32%
	FTE increase	4

9.2.2 Change in Circumstances

This mode is one of two actual production batches and is run on a weekly basis. The difference between this mode of operation and regression testing is that the answers that were based on stored, old customer data are replaced by up-to-date customer data.

That way, changes in the situation of the customer are detected and reevaluated. Thus, not only changed rules but also changes in data will result in changed outcomes.

9.2.3 Pre-existing Scan

In this mode, customers without a prior stored risk detection check are reevaluated. As no stored answers can be used, only the available customer data is used.

Because it is impossible to assess each customer, this scan picks out the customers with the highest priority. Rule changes and data changes may result in the need to assess those customers with an interview and follow-up investigation.

9.3 Risk model

The introduction of the current risk model consisted of an Excel file containing all risk indicators and their corresponding questions. The calculation rules used to determine the risk scores per indicator and the overall risk score were Excel formulas referencing values in different tabs of the Excel.

The many references and lookup-functions in the Excel made it very difficult to read, let alone maintain.

Below a small example of the complexity of this model:

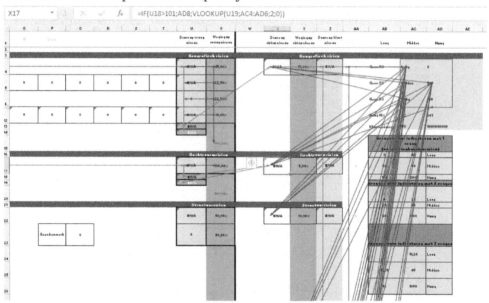

Because of the complexity of the model, the only way to ensure a rule-based model that returned the same outcomes as the Excel model, was to reengineer it and create an identical model in rule format. Using the Excel, we could create a regression test to verify whether the rules were sound and complete.

Another requirement of the model was that new questions should easily be added to the model. For this reason and for easy calculation purposes, all questions were represented by a question entity related to an indicator entity which in turn is related to the check entity.

The model has the following general structure:

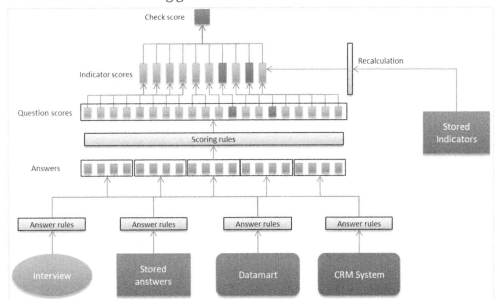

The overall check score is calculated by a weighted sum of the indicator scores which in turn are calculated by a weighted sum of the question scores.

The question scores are determined by scoring rules that assign a specific score to each possible answer. Some questions can be answered by selecting multiple countries or product types. In those cases, the highest risk score of each selected country or product is assigned to the question.

the risk indicator	the weight of the risk indicator
NPCDD00G	0,18
NPCDD03S	0,18
NPCDD04P	0,10
NPCDD05P	0,10
NPCDD06T	0,14
NPCDD07L	0,05
NPCDD08D	0,10
NPCDD09K	0,15
ORCDD00G	0,15
ORCDD01R	0,05
ORCDD02S	0,10
ORCDD03S	0,15
ORCDD04P	0,15
ORCDD05P	0,10
ORCDD06T	0,10
ORCDD07L	0,05
ORCDD08D	0,05
ORCDD09K	0,10
else	uncertain

The following are some examples of the calculation rules involved:

> [riskcalculation] **the risk score of the check = InstanceSum(all indicators; the weighted risk score of the risk indicator)**

> [riskcalculation] **the weighted risk score of the risk indicator = the risk score of the risk indicator * the weight of the risk indicator**

The table is an example of a simple rule table that assigns a weight to each indicator (green cells are conditions matching indicator ids; yellow cells are conclusions that set the correct weight)

Because the data coming from different systems has technically different structures and formats in each channel, a separate layer of answer rules are necessary to take care of the mapping between the data and a fixed set of possible answers known to the risk model.

9.4 Rules architecture

So far, we have a visible calculation model which is not typical for rule-based solutions. However, the calculation model is just the core in a wider set of rules.

For instance, based on the risk calculations, some rules are applied to determine if and which follow-up questions need to be asked in the follow-up investigation for medium- and high-risk customers. Below is an example rule:

the follow-up questions of Geografical risk NP wrt Money Laundering are relevant if

the assessment customer is a person and
either
the assessment customer is stateless or
ExistsScope(all countries)
the AML/TF-questionscore of the country = 1 and
the country has been selected under Geografical risk NP

The rules are written in compilable Word and Excel documents.

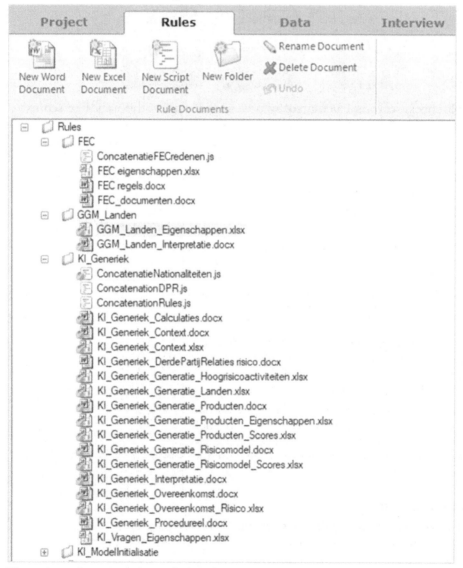

The rules refer to entities, relationships and attributes defined in a data model.

In total, the rule base contains the following number of rule documents, attributes and entities:

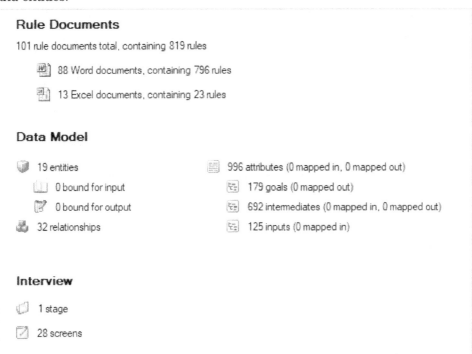

All these documents are ordered to subject of the rules:
- Generic:
  - model initialization
  - generic calculation rules
  - country rules
  - service request rules
  - product rules
- Per indicator:
  - Answer rules: map data (from any source including the screen) to model answers
  - Scoring rules: assign scores to selected model answers
  - Screen rules: default answers, visibility and enablement rules
- Routing rules: what business unit performs the follow-up investigation
- Follow-up questions: determine follow-up questions to ask

9.5 Inclusion structure

Each rule base can have only one data mapping to an external system, so for each channel a separate rule base is needed. To be able to reuse the same rules in each channel, the same set of rules has to be embedded in each rule base. The BRE facilitates modules of rules called inclusions that are normal rule bases and that can be included in other rule bases, thus enabling single point of definition.

The Customer Due Diligence-rule bases consist of three layers:
1. Basic rule bases for specific business objects and core business rules, including the risk model
2. Application rule bases, using different inclusions for interview, recalculation and batch
3. Integration rule bases, setting the mappings to different external systems, including separate mappings for Persons and Organizations.

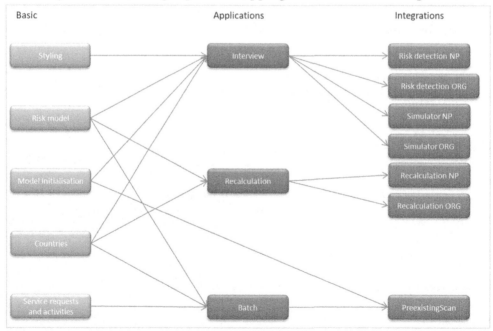

9.5 Business rules management

All development is administered using the issue tracking system Jira, using the SAFE agile framework. New and changed functionality is described in Themes, Epics, Features and User stories.

After the risk model was first implemented in the rules, rule management was still commencing. The business was still using the Excel risk model. Hence, also all changes were expressed in terms of the Excel implementation. This meant that these changes had to be looked up in the Excel first to see what the actual change consisted of. This was tedious and error prone.

The Rule team raised this several times as an issue, but there was still quite some distance between the IT department and the business unit responsible for policy. This situation came to end when the Excel actually did prove to be unmaintainable and could not be used anymore because of inconsistencies that were practically impossible to fix.

This together with organizational changes led to a situation where the business together with the product owner is more directly involved in the rule team. All incidents, issues, changes and new functionality and rules are discussed during a biweekly business review.

The agenda of the business reviews looks like this:

Operations
- Important production incidents

Development
- System demo built and tested features
- Impediments and outstanding questions
- Backlog refinement new features

Business
- Roadmap
- New business

Production incidents usually involve data integrity issues - such as missing addresses or nationality codes - which are still present from legacy systems, that later have been centralized and merged in the main CRM system. Data quality is being considered all the time, but all rule bases, especially batch rule bases, have to take into account lesser quality data. Only when no sensible decision can be made based on the available data or when data issues occur that have not been considered at all will an incident be raised.

User stories and features that are discussed during the business review may involve rules, obviously, but also all other components and relevant processes. Built and tested user stories are demoed and approved by the product owner and subsequently deployed to production.

When no incidents have occurred, the largest part of the time in the business review is spent on new and changing features under development. When any time is left, future developments are discussed or potential new innovations.

After intake of a RFC, a new feature and/or user stories will be added to the backlog. The team decides, conforming to scrum principles, whether or not the user stories will be pulled into a sprint.

9.5.1 Development, rule authoring

All rule bases reside on a development hub, in the repository section. The repository section is divided into multiple collections, each containing zero, one or more rule bases. User authorization is defined at collection level.

The hub and the rule authoring client facilitate collaboration using a versioning mechanism. All rule base documents are checked out automatically when opened and changed. When ready and tested locally, changes can be uploaded to the hub resulting in a new repository version of the rule base, which can subsequently be downloaded by other users. Potential conflicts are resolved by either reverting to the original version before downloading changes or by stealing ownership from another user (only when necessary as it would potentially throw away work done by the other user).

To ensure a smooth development process, guidelines are in effect for working with the client and the hub with regard to versioning. This process is also considered architecturally by finding a balance between one rule per document or all rules in one document; both would be unwieldy.

For rule authoring, guidelines are in place. On a confluence page, they are maintained. These guidelines are not many and have been added and improved through the years, based on experience.

To understand the guidelines for rule authors, one must have some basic knowledge of attribute definition in the business rule engine. An attribute is defined by its attribute text, datatype and name. The attribute text is what is used in the rules and shown on screens. The name is a technical identifier that is used for integration and logging purposes. Attributes are added automatically to the data model when writing rules but can also be defined manually. The following rule authoring guidelines are in effect:

1. At least every input and output attribute have a name.
2. Every attribute referencing a particular concept has an attribute text starting with a definite article ('the').
3. Every attribute, except global attributes, has an attribute text that contains the entity name the attribute belongs to.
   - Try to avoid more than one entity name in an attribute text
   - Follow the fact-type-model for known attributes
   - Preferred formats for attribute-texts are the following:
     - booleans: \<the entity> \<verb> \<noun phrase) | verb phrase | prepositional phrase>
       Examples:
       the customer is a person (verb + noun phrase)
       the customer has been registered (verb phrase)
       the customer throws a ball (verb + noun phrase)
       the customer is eligible (adjective (is also a noun phrase))
       the customer lives in the Netherlands (prepositional phrase)
     - value-attributes: \<the property> of \<the entity>, \<the entity>'s \<property>
       Example: the name of the customer, the customer's name
   - Attribute texts do not contain commas. (Commas disrupt proper formatting of a data model export.csv)
4. Capitals in attributes are only used when language spelling rules require them (e.g. names of people)

5. Descriptive comments are placed in an introductory paragraph preceding the rules in that paragraph
6. Change comments are placed in the change history on top of the rule document, at least containing:
   - the identifier of the user story that describes the requirements of the change
   - a reference to the rules that have been changed: either using the conclusion attribute of the particular rules or, when many rules have been changed, a reference to the particular ruleset (e.g. paragraph, chapter, document)
7. Relationship texts start with the target entity, use a verb phrase (possibly in genitivus) and end with the source entity. (using the full target and source entity names enables alias substitution)
8. Use of scope with multiple inner scope conditions suggests that you use an intermediate attribute at the inner scope level
9. Multiple occurrences of a combination of conditions suggests that you use an intermediate attribute as a substitute
10. Specific data values are always converted to a boolean attribute:
    the risk category of the check is high if
    the risk category of the check = "High"
11. No rule's condition section starts with a grouping operator unless the condition group is followed by one or more condition groups on the same level (F1)
    - No:
      this rule is wrong if
          both
              the rule starts with a condition and
              the rule has another condition
    - Yes:
      this rule is correct if
          the rule starts with a condition and
          the rule has another condition
      this rule is correct if
          both
              the rule starts with a condition and
              the rule has another condition
          or
          both
              the rule has third condition and
              the rule has fourth condition
12. All attributes are atomic: they convey only one property of an entity and do not combine multiple properties, because that would be a rule compressed in one attribute (which would require changing when the underlying rule changes)
    Combining conditions in the attribute text of an inferred attribute is to be avoided, unless necessary.
    - Wrong:
      the service request is an open client integrity service request with an incorrect plan date

- Correct:

  the service request is open and

  the service request is a client integrity service request and

  the plan date of the service request is incorrect

  Possible exceptions:

  the negation of an ExistsScope-operator with multiple conjunctive conditions would require converting it to a ForAllScope with multiple disjunctive conditions. This might be hard to read and might impact performance. In this case, it is easier to create a boolean based on the positive expression of the ExistsScope operator and use the negation of the Boolean. The boolean is preferably phrased as a separate property that makes sense to the business instead of an enumeration of all conditions.

13. Each rule author must uncheck the MS Word option to change normal quotes (single and double) to smart (curly) quotes.

Because the business rule engine is a production rule system, most rules are formulated in a positive, inferential style, contrary to a constraining style. Only validation rules are formulated in a style analogous to RuleSpeak. The most important consideration regarding formulation is that it is easily understandable. This principle is sometimes at odds with the complexity of the data and the logic.

9.5.2 Deployments

Besides a repository section, the hub also has a deployment section. From the client, a working rule base can be deployed to the hub. A deployment can be activated for three different interfaces: interview, web service or mobile. A deployment can also be downloaded and put into a batch configuration: the batch processor is a separate component that runs on a separate server.

At Rabobank, five hubs are used, a development hub, two test hubs, an acceptance hub and a production hub. Only the development hub holds a repository section, the other four only contain deployments. One test hub is always synchronized with the production hub, the other test hub follows development.

When a new deployment is activated, running interview sessions will keep running on the prior deployment. New sessions will use the new deployment. Interview sessions that are resumed will do so in the new version. This may be problematic as the impact on the interview of changes in the rule base may be too large to resume the interview. The BRE decides whether an interview can sensibly be resumed. If not possible, then the user will be shown a message that the interview has to be restarted.

9.5.3 Operations

Once in production, and no incidents occur, there is still some work to do for the team. The weekly batches are scheduled and only need to be checked on successful completion (automated controls are being developed), but ad hoc batches are started and monitored manually. Furthermore, reporting is still done manually as requirements for automated reporting have not been formulated yet.

9.6 Traceability

The Dutch National Bank requires banks to be able to show how they comply to the WWFT. Rabobank ensures this by invoking an internal audit. One of the benefits of using explicit rules is an almost one-on-one correspondence between the regulations, in this case the Customer Due Diligence-standards, and the rules.

During the audit, it was possible to answer all questions the internal audit team had by showing the rules that covered the particular subject of the questions.

Furthermore, after the audit, the rule team proposed to have a more explicit link between the rules and the Customer Due Diligence standards and such is currently under development. The rule authoring client facilitates rule tagging by placing text between square brackets before a rule conclusion or a rule condition, like in the following example (in Dutch).

```
[2.1.1 Vereenvoudigd klantonderzoek] de te beoordelen klant is een overheidsinstelling als
        voor(de te beoordelen klant; de klant is een overheidsinstelling)


[2.1.1 Vereenvoudigd klantonderzoek] de klant is een overheidsinstelling als
        bestaatbereik(de bedrijfsindelingen voor de klant)
                de bedrijfsindeling staat voor een overheidsinstelling


[2.1.1 Vereenvoudigd klantonderzoek] de bedrijfsindeling staat voor een overheidsinstelling als
        de bedrijfsindeling code is gegeven en
        een van volgende
                de bedrijfsindeling code = "841100" of
                de bedrijfsindeling code = "841200" of
                de bedrijfsindeling code = "841300" of
                de bedrijfsindeling code = "842100" of
                de bedrijfsindeling code = "842200" of
                de bedrijfsindeling code = "842310" of
                de bedrijfsindeling code = "842320" of
                de bedrijfsindeling code = "842400" of
                de bedrijfsindeling code = "842500" of
                de bedrijfsindeling code = "843000" of
                de bedrijfsindeling code = "843002" of
                de bedrijfsindeling code = "843003" of
                de bedrijfsindeling code = "843004"
```

The tag references a paragraph in the Customer Due Diligence standards explaining that a simplified assessment is applicable for government institutions. The tags can be used in the search box of the tool to find all rule documents that refer to that particular paragraph.

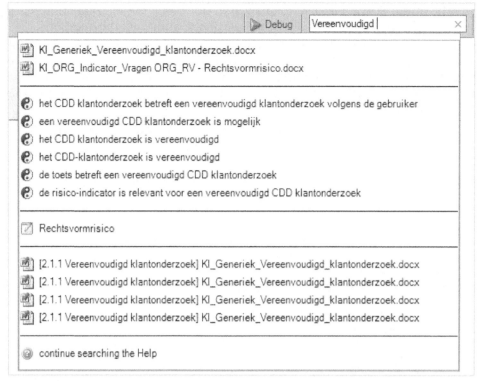

The tags also appear in the debugger when conclusions or conditions have been tagged. In the debugger, decisions and their dependencies can be viewed as a decision tree. The tags are shown beside each corresponding condition or conclusion in italic. When clicked, the relevant rule documents and rules appear in a pop up.

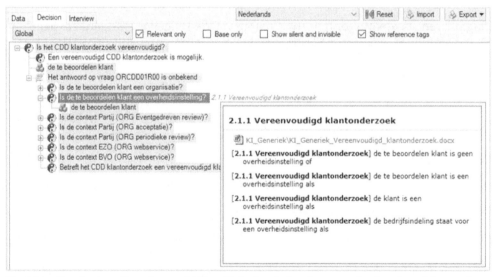

Besides the design-time traceability, Rabobank is also required to be able to show why decisions have been made, ie. what rules have been applied at the time of the decision for a particular customer, and what is called part of the audit trail.

This is runtime traceability and has been implemented by adding a timestamp and a risk model version to each check record that is stored. With these data items, specific decisions can always be traced back to the applicable rule base version. An improvement to this would be to store the actual decision reports that can be generated by the rule engine.

9.7 Testing

The rule team distinguishes the following types testing:

- Logical regression test: all logic is tested by rerunning a regression test with more than 1.000 test cases.
- System test: being able to run the system in different modes (interview service, web-service, batch)
- Integration test: running the system + various functional and technical tests to verify integration/mappings
- UI-test local: interview walkthrough in the debugger of the rule authoring tool
- UI-test server: interview walkthrough in the CRM-system

9.7.1 Regression testing

The aforementioned test-cases are contained in Excel test-scripts. Each test-script contains a N number of cases. A test-case contains input columns for each attribute in each entity that needs data (each entity has a separate worksheet and references to instantiations of other entities).

A test-case contains expected value columns to compare actual derived values with expected value. On the general (global) test-sheet, all cases are listed and have PASS/FAIL column. When one of the derived values does not match the corresponding expected value, the corresponding cell in the PASS/FAIL column will turn red and show FAIL. Otherwise, it will be green and show PASS.

To be able to analyze why a test-case has failed, the debugger can be started from the selected test-case and will be pre-seeded with the data from the particular test-case. Subsequently, all inferences that have or have not been made can be checked, until one typically finds a value that has not been set or that is incorrect or a rule that has been misconstructed.

Because the more than thousand test-cases also contain expected values for all calculated risk-scores at question, indicator and check level, only a slight deviation in the test-case will immediately trigger a fail.

This has enabled us to keep up a high-quality standard: every change is first regression tested to see the impact on the risk model. For certain changes, some test-cases are expected to fail. Then the new expected values are entered and when the test-cases pass in the second run, the change is approved. When other then expected test-cases fail, a more in-depth analysis is performed.

Example clip from a test-script:

Test	Results	de te beoordel en klant	de gebruiker heeft bevestigd dat geen woonlanden zijn	de landen waar de klant de afgelopen 3 jaar heeft gewoond	de risicoscore van het geografisch risico N	de risicocategor ie van het geografisch risico NP	de bepaalde risicoscore
1	PASS	1	TRUE	""	50	Midden	9,00
2	PASS	2	TRUE	""	50	Midden	9,00
3	PASS	3	FALSE	XX	100	Hoog	70,00
4	PASS	4	TRUE	""	284	Hoog	103,12
5	PASS	5	FALSE	YY	284	Hoog	51,12
6	PASS	6	TRUE	""	284	Hoog	103,12
7	PASS	7	FALSE	YY	284	Hoog	103,2
8	PASS	8	TRUE	""	100	Hoog	18,00
9	PASS	9	TRUE	""	50	Midden	9,00
10	PASS	10	FALSE	ZZ	100	Hoog	18,00
11	PASS	11	FALSE	AA	50	Midden	9,00
12	PASS	12	TRUE	""	50	Midden	9,00
13	PASS	13	FALSE	BB	284	Hoog	51,12

10. THE TECHNOLOGY AND SERVICE PROVIDERS

10.1 Customer involvement, Service providers and consultants

Rabobank, Sales and Client Processes

www.rabobank.nl

- Joel Meyer, Lead Product Manager
- Martijn Hagens, Senior Delivery Manager
- Saskia van der Toorn, Product Manager
- Ralph van de Rijt, Delivery Manager
- Jacco Willemse, COO Customer Due Diligence Service Centrum
- Arthur Rotgers, Senior Compliance Expert CAMS, CO GC AML & Sanctions
- Eric Stout, Solution Architect Client Processes
- Edwin Cornelissen, Lead Business Analyst Sales and Client Processes

Oracle Netherlands

www.oracle.com/nl

- Martijn Tromm, Lead OPA Rules Architect and Application Engineer
- Evert Kroon, OPA Rules Architect
- Tim Janssens, OPA Consultant
- Martin Bower, Technical Director Siebel
- Pieter Jan 't Hoen, OPA Team lead Benelux

IBM

http:///www.ibm.com/nl

- Marco Leeflang, Scrum master and OPA Consultant
- Marc Herni, OPA Consultant and Tester
- Emidio da Costa Gomez, OPA Consultant and Siebel specialist
- Jan Schuddeboom, Siebel Specialist
- Paul Blakey, Siebel Specialist

Freelancers

- Marten Schokking, Business Analyst, OPA Consultant, Siebel specialist
- Richard Simons, OPA Consultant and Tester
- Frederik Meerens, OPA Consultant

10.2 Technology

- Oracle Policy Automation, v12.2.9
- Oracle Policy Modeling, v12.2.9
- Oracle Database 11g
- Oracle Siebel IP2016

10.3 Authors BREA Submission

- Marten Schokking
- Martijn Tromm

Traffic Control, The Netherlands
Nominated by LibRT, The Netherlands

1. EXECUTIVE SUMMARY / ABSTRACT

Rule-based traffic management is a methodology for dynamic traffic management that is a joint development of the different road authorities (municipal, state, central government) in the Netherlands and the major suppliers of the road authorities.

Traffic managers used flow charts to describe what the traffic operator should do in response to an event like congestion during rush hour, an accident or football match. With thousands of flowcharts to maintain, each infrastructure change would result in the need to update many flowcharts. The situation was beholding the road authorities to innovate while the industry is working on new technologies (connected cars, IOT) to communicate with the road user.

A better way is using declarative business rules that describe what must, may and can be done to improve a traffic situation. Typically, we promote the outbound flow, decrease inbound flow or reroute traffic. The new approach is simple, easy to maintain and connected to the policies agreed between the road authorities in a region.

A prerequisite of automated execution is the availability of actual and reliable traffic data. A national data center collects and distributes traffic data of different sources. Road authorities use this data to execute the automated rules.

The results show that traffic is successfully distributed across the road network and congestion is prevented. The feedback of operators in the traffic management center is positive. They believe the approach simplifies their work, they trust and understand the methodology and they have more time to handle complex situations like incidents.

2. OVERVIEW

The road authorities for an area have agreed on a joint vision about traffic management resulting in: the selection of roads that are available for traffic management, the preferred and diversion routes for the most important traffic flows based on analyses of origin-destination flows, road priority to indicate which roads should

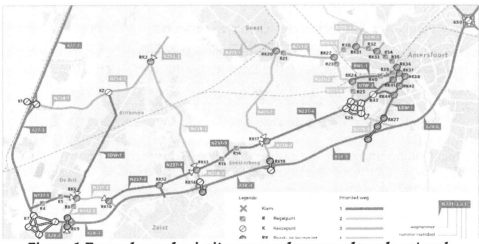

Figure 1 Example road priority map and managed roads network.

have good traffic flow conditions, eventually at the expense of other (lower priority) roads in the network (see an example in figure 1) and threshold values to classify a traffic situation as a bottleneck (traffic management norms).

Traffic managers influence traffic conditions requesting one of the following traffic services:

- **Increase outbound flow** – a service that controls traffic capacity at a flow control point, thus enhancing the amount of traffic that can exit a link in a given direction. For example, longer green light times for outbound traffic.

- **Decrease inbound flow** – a service that controls traffic capacity at a flow control point, thus restricting the amount of traffic that can enter the link from a specific upstream link. For example, longer red light times for inbound traffic.

- **Reroute** – a service that directs traffic from a destination to a diversion route at a decision point. For example, a reroute advise on an electronic display.

Typically, each service changes a setting in a traffic control device like a traffic light or an electronic display but upcoming new IoT devices, which directly communicate with the environment, may also be involved.

The rule-based traffic management (RBTM) is based on four principles that determine which service must be requested. First, we want to prevent saturation on a road by early detection of bottlenecks and request of services to control outbound and inbound traffic. Next, we want to optimize travel time by requesting the reroute services. Third, compliance with the policy constraints set by the traffic management authority must be guaranteed. Finally, the most severe traffic situation prevails when conflicting services are requested.

A traffic operator needs guidance to execute these principles. Therefore, each principle translates to a set of generic business rules that answer questions like: Which traffic management service must be requested? Is a traffic management service available? Which traffic management service must be executed when conflicting services are requested?

The business rules are based on the thresholds set by the traffic management norm on a link or route segment and the priority of roads, taking practical considerations, like the availability of traffic data, into account. The business rules are presented as decision tables that follow the semantics defined in the standard 'Decision Model Notation' [3] as 'rules as cross-tab' or 'rules as columns'.

WHICH KIND OF SERVICE TO REQUEST?

Problem phase:	Saturation	Congestion	Gridlock
Promote outbound?	Request	Request	Request
Limit inbound?	-	Request	Request
Reroute?	-	-	Request

For each link and route segment, the operational traffic engineer must create business rules that define the problem phase of a traffic situation. Table 2 shows a generic version of this logic.

WHAT IS THE PROBLEM PHASE?			
Topology:	*Link*	*Link*	*Route segment*
Waiting queue:	*>90% of sorting lane*	*>90% of link*	-
Travel time:	-	-	*> 90% of travel time norm*
Saturation?	Yes	-	-
Congestion?	No	Yes	-
Gridlock?	No	No	Yes

The order in which the business rules and traffic situations are evaluated is defined by the process logic and typically executed by a Traffic Management System. When all business rules are evaluated, the service requests will be executed and the process restarts (see figure 2). Services may also be started manually by a traffic operator based. In that case, the traffic operator is also responsible to terminate a service. The service availability conditions are still to be respected.

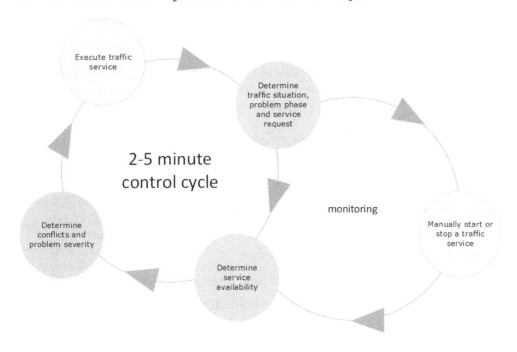

Figure 2 Visualization of the process logic

3. BUSINESS CONTEXT

The road networks in the Netherlands are, together with those of the Scandinavian countries, among the safest in the world. One of the factors contributing to this position is the attention paid to road safety in traffic management processes and systems. Significant parts of both networks have automated queue protection. The network has a relatively high traffic density (about 20 million vehicle kilometers per motorway kilometer per year) over the whole highway network, with (much) higher densities in metropolitan areas. Inductive loop detectors to measure traffic passages, matrix traffic signals, traffic signs and dynamic route information panels are used extensively. Distances between junctions and interchanges are short and speed limits are not uniform.

There are five regional traffic control centers for managing the highways, tunnels and bridges (see figure 3). The 13 provinces have traffic control centers for managing the regional roads. There are 100 municipalities but only the larger cities (Amsterdam, Rotterdam, The Hague, Utrecht) have traffic control centers to manage the urban roads.

Figure 3 Control centers

Response plans are used for mutual agreement, communication and control of the desired response to specific traffic events. A response plan translates policy and experience in operational instructions, often in the form of a flow chart (see figure 4). Response plans are intended for human operators to deal with events, incidents and road works. Response plans are typically executed by Traffic Management Systems of multiple authorities.

In the last decade response plans have also been developed for daily traffic management. The broad use of response plans has resulted in a labor-intensive maintenance and operational execution process. Many response plans are needed for different locations and situations (e.g., morning rush, evening rush, forecast event, incident, roadwork). Each response plan details: problem detection, problem solution in terms of the setting of signs and signals, handling of conflicting requests for a traffic control device, and restoring to 'normal'.

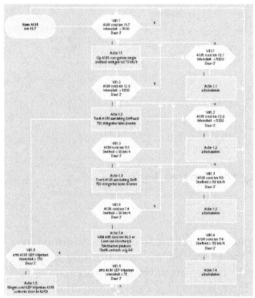

Figure 4 Flow chart response plan

4. THE KEY INNOVATIONS

The main objective of Rule Based Traffic Management (RBTM) is to develop a more efficient process to facilitate and execute daily operational traffic management, thus enhancing quality and effectiveness. Additional benefits of the standardization of traffic management rules are an easier transition to new technologies (like in-car systems) and tightening of the connection between traffic policy and operational execution (compliance).

4.1 Proven Business and Operational Impact

The approach is evaluated in two pilot projects. The first project evaluated the results of the approach for improved traffic flow on the highway ring-road of Amsterdam. The results showed that traffic flow on the highway improved at the expense of traffic conditions on the urban roads. A second pilot evaluated how the approach could distribute the traffic on the network by extending the approach to more services on the provincial and urban roads.

The evaluation was performed on a network of roads in the North of Amsterdam, consisting of the westbound traffic on N516, starting with the intersection N203 (provincial road), until its junction with the A8 (highway). The network has seven traffic lights, one ramp meter and one bridge. This network was chosen because there is an overloaded intersection that connects with the urban roads to a satellite city (Zaandam) causing many traffic jams. The situation is very typical for other locations in the Netherlands. The new approach was active for 40 days. The results from this time period have been compared to the traffic situation on days where the traffic lights have the 'typically most optimal' program.

The results show that the number of vehicle loss hours is slightly improved (four percent) during rush hours. More importantly, the traffic problem is distributed to lower priority roads in the network by showing increased vehicle loss hours and longer waiting queues on these roads, resulting in an improved compliance with the policy. The net result is improved traffic flow.

These results are confirmed by showing an expected decrease in rear-end collisions but there is also an increase in red light runners. This is an undesired but natural result of the service 'decrease inbound flow'. The average satisfaction score of the road users is also significantly better on the days where the rule approach was 'on' as shown in Figure 4. The blue line indicates whether the rule approach was 'on' (1) or 'off' (0). The red line shows the average road user satisfaction. It follows the same pattern as the blue line indicating that the road user satisfaction increases when the rule approach was 'on'.

The results of week 52 are not representative due to a holiday in this week. There is no statistically significant other explanation for the increase in the road user satisfaction than the improved traffic conditions due to the rule approach being 'on' [Figure 5].

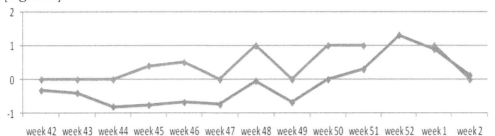

Figure 5 Road user satisfaction analysis

The Netherlands is a country with a high population density and a road network that is used to its full capacity with little options to change the infrastructure. Therefore, spectacular results in the improvement of the traffic situation are very hard to achieve, causing small but significant improvements to be recognized. This approach demonstrated improved service of the road authority to the road user by improving the traffic flow on high priority roads and increased road user satisfaction. These results contribute directly to the mission of the road authority to provide safe roads with reliable traffic times to the public. The traffic engineers have less work to maintain the conditions for requesting traffic management services and the approach can be fully automated (see section 4.3).

Feedback of the traffic operators is that the approach is much easier to understand because it is standardized for each situation. We believe this standardization also contributed to an improvement in the way different road authorities collaborate. Now that we are implementing the approach, we see that the major improvements in traffic conditions result from this collaboration.

Finally, we recently see that employees change jobs and move from one road authority to another. Although we do not know if this is a direct result of the standardized way of working and increased collaboration between the road authorities, it is a desired result because it makes the market for traffic operators more flexible. When one region has more work due to an event it will be easier to attract temporarily more traffic operators without the need of a long training program in a local way of working.

4.2 Innovation

The new approach separates the management of the road network (using the generic business rules) and the management of road side equipment (like traffic lights and electronic messaging signs). This paves the road to easily connect to innovations that are changing our world rapidly.

Instead of communicating a reroute service to road users by setting a text on a dynamic route information panel on a fixed location, we may broadcast the reroute service directly to the navigation system, a connected car or other smart device that is in a certain area.

These location aware smart devices, could also send information back. Traffic engineers could better anticipate, for example, when they know how many road users take the detour or what the destination and purpose is of a trip. The Dutch program 'Talking Traffic' and European program 'Socrates' are examples where collaboration with the automotive industry is explored by exchanging policy and service request information from the rule-based approach to traffic management with service providers of navigation software.

So, by standardizing the network management layer, we have also created a way to standardize the communication about our policy with other parties. This is a requirement for adopting the technology innovation since the technology changes, not the policy.

4.3 Impact and Implementation

We believe the multi agent systems approach is applicable to similar domains that deal with flows in time; for example, crowd management during an event or passenger flows in a museum. The terminology for traffic situations and services may need to be slightly adjusted for those domains. Also, the sensor data and actuator actions will be different. But the general idea of the standard decision logic for service request, service availability and service conflicts are likely to hold.

Currently, we are applying a similar approach to distributing capacity bottlenecks in an airport. The end-to-end airport process typically has more stakeholders (air traffic control, apron control, ground handling, customs, baggage handling, crowd management etc.). Typically, they each make their own planning that will be adjusted on the day of operations to deal with changes and disruptions.

The data needed to establish the traffic situation in the complete passenger and aircraft process chain becomes readily available. Airports have more and more means to gather information about the travelling process and start to realize that they are not only an 'air-hub' but also a data-hub. Smart use of this data may improve the travel experience for the customer and capacity of the airport.

The challenge is this domain is again to connect all the different stakeholders. Each of them (air control center, airport, airline, handler, security and customs) may have capacity issues and be the source for a major gridlock situation. Like the road authorities, each stakeholder has its own objectives and is used to make its own plan. This plan may be optimal for them but sub-optimal for the end-to-end process. It is again a challenge to align the stakeholders and agree on common value drivers.

Recent presentations of the methodology to a broad audience working in different domains taught us that the methodology is inspiring for processes in retail (logistics) and the finance industry (money flows). We are looking forward to applying this strategy to other domains and generalizing the methodology applied.

The applied methodology to standardize the process of policy compliance may also be extended to other domains. The general idea is to create a high-level vocabulary in terms of events and actions. These are combined using standard decision logic. A domain expert uses this as a framework to configure domain definitions. This way, the domain expert does not need to work on algorithmic logic himself and instead finds his way more easily in a system of rules.

5. Hurdles Overcome

After the bill on a kilometer tax to decrease traffic on rush hours was rejected, the minister of infrastructure gave the road authorities the assignment to collaborate and use the existing road network capacity in an optimal way. This included the idea of distributing traffic over the whole road network. However, each road authority was used to doing traffic management in their own way, with their own methodology and local experts. The first meetings on collaboration turned out to be a school example of misunderstanding, underestimation and complaints.

4.1 Management

The first challenge was to agree that a common methodology was feasible and desired. We organized ten workshops with 20 representatives of different road authorities resulting in a description of the current practices and the desired practice in road management. It was far from being a complete methodology and the number of concepts having multiple synonyms was too large. However, the first steps were taken and the following year, a second set of workshops with five representatives of different road authorities was organized, resulting in a description of a common vocabulary for network-based traffic management. The method was accepted as the standard approach by the national traffic council with representatives of different road authorities.

4.2 Business

The methodology is 'data hungry' in a sense that we need reliable and up to date data about traffic speed, traffic intensity and waiting queues. Therefore, the availability of cheaper ways to collection data, like floating car data, are essential for the methodology to be adopted. However, since this data is relatively new, we need to experiment with algorithms that interpret the data stream into meaningful and reliable information. These developments take time and slow down the adoption of the rule-based traffic management approach.

The quality of the traffic data in terms of reliability and accuracy is another prerequisite for automated execution of the approach. For a larger road network involving multiple road authorities with different budget constraints, this may be a challenge. The Dutch government has been investing for many years in a national datacenter that collects and distributes the traffic data from different sources. Quality issues have been resolved but it is a continuous challenge to monitor the quality and resolve issues.

4.3 Organization Adoption

To agree with 100 municipalities, 13 provinces and one central road authority on a new methodology for traffic management is already an achievement. The next challenge is organizational: employees must be trained, systems must be reconfigured, managers must understand the need, results must be evaluated, best practices must be shared, and guidelines must be up-to-date. Who will be in charge for this task? Our next challenge is to find an owner of the methodology that takes care of all these aspects.

Meanwhile, we organize three workshops per year to share experiences between the road authorities when they are implementing the new approach. Each region has selected a small section of the road network to implement the approach. As we speak, there are five of these implementation projects in progress. They all report similar improvements. This increases the confidence of traffic engineers to increase the size of the network that implements this approach.

6. BENEFITS

The benefits for road owners are related to lower labor costs and less investments in infrastructure. The benefits for road users are related to traffic time and safety.

6.1 Cost Savings / Time Reductions

All regions report an improvement in the overall capacity throughput of the infrastructure. As explained in section 4.1 in detail, this is measured by the decrease in number of vehicle loss hours of the network. Improvements between 4 and 18 percent are reported during rush hours. In practice, this means that the traffic flow on high priority roads is improved and traffic is distributed over more roads in the road network. A better usage of existing infrastructure means that we need less investments in new infrastructure. The cost of road infrastructure development in the Netherlands is between 10 and 50 million Euro per kilometer so cost savings may quickly result in high numbers depending on the specific local situation.

Benefits for road users may be calculated by using the cost for extra petrol due to traffic congestion for a road user of 1.11 Euro per hour. But there is also an economic cost of traffic congestion, especially for the logistics sector. The estimated cost of traffic congestion for the economy is 11.27 Euro per hour. A 4 percent reduction in vehicle loss hours during rush hour for a road that has an average traffic intensity of 2700 vehicles per hour the total cost savings can thus be calculated as $0.04 * 11.27 + 1.11) * 2700 * 4 = 5,348$ Euro per day per kilometer. For an average region, this can easily result in cost savings of 10 million Euro per year.

The improvements have not resulted in more incidents or compromised safety, therefore the traffic time reliability for the road user is still the same.

6.2 Increased Revenues

All regions experience that the first implementation of the approach requires a learning phase for all stakeholders, increased efforts to gather traffic data and improve data quality. The desired decrease in the number of labor hours is therefore not yet realized. However, it is expected that once the approach is fully implemented for the whole network and supported by agent-based rule technology (see section 9) a reduction of labor cost will be realized.

6.3 Quality Improvements

The rule-based traffic management approach relies more on automated requests of traffic services based on traffic data and less on a traffic operator that monitors the traffic. As a result, the decision biases of operators have less impact in the operations and it is not possible to 'forget' to request a service when dealing with multiple incidents and events at the same time. Although the number of missed opportunities by traffic operators have not been measured in advance, they themselves believe this approach helps them to deliver a better-quality result.

7. BEST PRACTICES, LEARNING POINTS AND PITFALLS

7.1 Best Practices and Learning Points

✓ *Common terminology is a requirement for successful collaboration in a value chain.*

✓ *The 80 / 20 rule has been successfully applied: simplify the decision criteria for the majority of decisions such that people have more time to work on the 'specials' for event and incident management.*

✓ *Decision tables are easy to understand, also by the operational level.*

✓ *Involve the responsible business owners from the start in the development of a new approach.*

✓ *Take time to evaluate and fine tune a new decision-making approach, even if the first results are not positive.*

✓ *Make sure there is a feedback loop to improve the approach.*

7.2 Pitfalls

✗ *In a complex value chain that consists of different juridical entities, it is difficult to find a responsible owner for the complete process.*

✗ *We were lucky that the policy was already highly formalized. When applying the same method in other domains, this may not be the case and more initial effort may be needed to connect the operational and policy level and ensure automatic compliance.*

✗ *A technology independent methodology has advantages in the long run but slows down the implementation phase.*

8. COMPETITIVE ADVANTAGES

For many centuries, the Netherlands has been a center for world trade. With two significant European cargo main ports, Schiphol airport and Port of Rotterdam, less that one hour distant from each other, the Netherlands is a key logistics hub for the through-transportation of goods to the European hinterland, making it an attractive location for foreign companies.

Logistics also plays a crucial role for virtually all other sectors; from the transportation of raw materials, right through to finished products. With a value added of 55 billion euros/year and 813.000 employees, the Logistics sector is a strong driver of the Dutch economy.

It is no surprise that the road to and from the harbor has the highest road priority. When traffic stops at this road, it may have consequences for the turnover processes in the harbor. Therefore, the rule-based methodology for traffic management provides the Netherlands with a major competitive advantage compared to other European countries.

9. TECHNOLOGY

The rule-based approach for traffic management is an implementation of a multi-agent system (MAS) [6] that deploys complex behavior based on simple rules. Each agent represents a link in the road network and has the goal to optimize the used capacity on its link.

Each agent is a model-based reflex agent [7]. Sensor information from the link (the environment) is translated to an assessment of the traffic situation on the link. Based on that assessment and the rules in the decision tables, one or more services are selected for a related point in the network. This service will send an action to an actuator. The actuator will change the environment and the agents on upstream and downstream links will react on those changes with the same strategy.

The methodology is different from earlier agent-based control mechanisms [8] in the domain of traffic management because they optimize multiple traffic lights on one intersection while we optimize a traffic network consisting of different kinds of roads (highways, regional roads and urban roads) using different kinds of actuators (traffic lights, ramp metering, dynamic speed, and rerouting). To our knowledge, this is the first large scale implementation of such a multi-agent strategy in traffic management.

10. THE TECHNOLOGY AND SERVICE PROVIDERS

The rule-based approach to traffic management is a methodology and is technology-independent. The need for a technology-independent approach arose from the fact that each road authority has its own IT budget, IT supplier and traffic management system (TMS).

We have successfully automated the approach with systems from three different suppliers. All suppliers support some kind of conditions – action rule language to configure the product. The amount of work and to configure and maintain the implementation differs per vendor but is generally perceived as 'too high'. The vendors do not support the idea of generic rules per link hence the decision logic needs to be replicated in the system for each link in the road network. Also, the distinction we make between criteria to request a service and criteria to stop a service is not supported by all vendors. Again, this results in duplications in the decision logic.

Some traffic engineers describe the situation as a 'maintenance nightmare'. It is therefore very likely that we will be asking the vendors to enhance their software to support the approach in a more user-friendly way or look for other software suppliers. A forward chaining object-oriented rule engine would be perfectly capably to implement the approach in an efficient way.

References

[1] OMG , "Decision Model and Notation standard," 2014. [Online].

[2] R. Krikke, "Evaluatierapport PPA noord," 2017. [Online]. Available: http://www.praktijkproefamsterdam.nl.

[3] Arcadis, "Evaluatie rapport praktijkproef amsterdam," [Online]. Available: http://www.praktijkproefamsterdam.nl.

[4] S. Spreeuwenberg and R. Gerrits, "Requirements for Successful Verification in Practice," *Proceedings Fifteenth Flairs conference,* pp. p 221, 2002.

[5] J. Cullen and A. Bryman, "The Knowledge Acquisition Bottleneck: Time for Reassessment?," *Expert Systems,* 1988.

[6] J. Ferber, Multi-Agent System: An Introduction to Distributed Artificial Intelligence, Harlow: Addison Wesley Longman, 1999.

[7] S. Russell and P. Norvig, Artificial Intelligence: A Modern Approach, New Jersey: Prentice Hall, 2003.

[8] F.-Y. Wang, " Agent-based control for networked traffic management systems," 2005.

United Services Automobile Association (USAA), United States

1. EXECUTIVE SUMMARY / ABSTRACT

Several years ago, USAA, Property & Casualty Company, embarked on a journey to engineer and document our business rules to capture intellectual capital and preserve corporate memory. After all, the business should know what the business is doing. The building of a business rules repository is an investment that takes time and people, and in the end, its value is priceless. Our users of a business rules repository are vast - underwriters, product managers, defect managers, development and execution owners, experience owners, insurance compliance owners, competitive intelligence owners and quality assurance analysts. Some of the benefits a repository provides are:

- Faster time to market for adjusting existing products or creating new ones
- Ability to respond to market conduct exams confidently and efficiently
- Promotes compliance
- Identification of defects and provision of quicker resolutions
- Improved transference of business knowledge

In addition to engineering business rules, the team has begun exploring system architecture to provide further benefit to our users. Including business rules in a system architecture model at points where they impact processes broadens the user's understanding of the business as a whole.

2. OVERVIEW

It is imperative for a company to know what the business is doing. To accomplish this, business professionals must take responsibility for knowing what the business does. The project quite simply was to build a business rules repository. Some of the steps to reach that end goal included: Building a team of people with the right skill set and passion about building a rules repository

- Securing executive sponsorship
- Defining the target market
  - Who will be using the repository?
  - Why will they be using it?
  - What information do they expect to receive?
  - How will they expect to receive the information?
- Conducting interviews of potential users to enlist their help on what topics they'd most like to see documented first
- Developing a business modeling methodology
- Developing a road map of the work to be accomplished as prioritized by users in the interviews
- Listening to the concerns of potential users – especially about the ability to find information easily and ensuring the information is current and correct
- Researching best practices of writing rules and defining terms
- Engaging business rules training
- Creating a cross-functional team of people to review proposed terms and their definitions

- Investigating and selecting a rules repository tool – especially one that is compliant with Semantics for Business Vocabulary and Rules (SBVR)
- Marketing the repository and its benefits to users
- Injecting business rules in the project world
- Developing a governance process

Some of the benefits realized by developing a business rules repository are:

Development and execution – Having immediate access to knowledge of the current state saves time and money vs. a prolonged research effort to re-create the information which wastes valuable project time and money. A project can save as much as 40 percent of the project budget and time just by using the business rules and system architecture vs. having IT mine the code for the information.

Compliance - The number of market conduct exams by state departments of insurance is increasing. Having an available repository of business rules enables a faster response to an examiner's request, whereas in the past, that same information had to be compiled from a variety of sources. Another benefit realized while researching and developing the rules occurred when the team identified some inconsistencies between various resources in the validation process, thereby enabling proactive realignment between intent and implementation of potential issues.

Knowledge expansion and transference - Historically, it is not uncommon to have only a couple of subject matter experts for a given aspect of the business. A business rules repository makes the information accessible to a wide audience. When roles shift, the business rules are used as a training tool, enabling faster knowledge transfer to a new subject matter expert.

Preservation of corporate memory – Knowledge regarding how our business is run was traditionally contained within the minds of individual business professionals. With an increase in people retiring and the usual turnover from people seeking new opportunities, the potential to lose the knowledge and experience accumulated over the years becomes all too real. Documenting the business rules in order to prevent this loss of corporate memory is invaluable.

Defect resolution – Business rules help to determine if the system is performing as intended, and if not, they enable a quick solution.

Greater business agility – Cost reduction, time savings and reduced time to market are all possible with the documentation of business rules. For example, a project budgeted and planned four weeks to develop a set of requirements, part of which included time to research and understand the current state. Upon learning this, two business rules team members were able to provide the project team a completed set of business rules within a matter of a couple of hours. As a result, the business requirements were completed in only three hours and the system requirements were completed in the first week: an incredible 75 percent decrease in the original time and cost allotted.

Improves clarity and consistency – Everyone has encountered a set of project requirements and thought "is it any wonder why things were not implemented as the business meant". Sometimes what is intended is simply not clear. Engineering business rules using a specific methodology based on SBVR provides clarity in the rules and consistency amongst business rules analysts in how they are written, thereby greatly reducing ambiguity and incorrect implementation.

Unfortunately, not everything goes along smoothly. Some of the challenges were:

- **Securing executive support** – This step is absolutely required to be successful at building a business rules repository. There were periods when executive support was not as strong as needed—usually due to a personnel change-- and the priority of building a repository waned. When this happens, meeting with executives to explain the benefits of a repository is crucial to success.

- **Business buy-in** – The majority of people in business that hear the business rules story agree on the importance and the need to engineer and document business rules. To accomplish this, you need support from end-users and management. The team met with executives and brought in respected experts in the business rules community to share their wisdom. Within the company, our IT partners were a tremendous help with conveying the importance of a business rules repository. We communicated the time needed for this type of effort and the benefits a rule repository would provide in the end. Continued communication helped awareness grow and so did the Business support, who began sharing the importance and benefits of business rules with others helping to spread the word even more quickly for our team.

- **Infiltrating the project world** – It took some time and proof of concept, but eventually business rules proved themselves in being a valuable part of implementing a project. In the past, the company was using the waterfall approach and business rules became a mandatory artifact. Recently, the company began using an agile approach to development and execution of changes and the business rules management team is working to find the right place in this model.

3. BUSINESS CONTEXT

The impetus for beginning our business rules journey was the replacement of a legacy IT system. The business needed to be able to act faster to changes and the legacy system did not enable that. The company embarked on a multi-year project that included a discussion on business rules. Certainly, there were procedures, manuals, specifications, and subject matter experts but not a single source or business rules. In the beginning, the business did not have much information or knowledge about business rules and IT was the primary area lobbying for them. Researching and discovering experts, information and conferences provided the groundwork. As the business rules team learned more, we thought the same thing Ron Ross always says, "Why isn't everyone doing this?" Imagine, a single source of the truth – business rules!

4. THE KEY INNOVATIONS

4.1 Business and Operational Impact

Increased revenues – While building our business rule repository, it did not result in a direct increase in revenues, the ability to accelerate time to market enables more development and innovation with faster implementation in an agile environment.

Proven importance to the organization's mission, vision, or goals – In order to fulfil the USAA mission of providing our members with a full-range of highly competitive products and services, the company has to be ready. Ready to adjust and move swiftly to implementation. Documentation of business rules provides current and future reference.

Enhanced consistency of business outcomes, decisions, or customer experience – There are a variety of users looking at rules, referencing them to obtain better clarity and understanding before making decisions that may impact business outcomes or customer experiences. They are often used to understand the current state, ensure compliance and speed time to market.

Establishment or improvement of compliance capabilities or traceability – Business rules have been utilized to support requests that arise from market conduct exams.

Improved understandability, accessibility, or reusability of business rules or decisions:

Understandability – Incorporation of feedback from users facilitates greater comprehension and usability for all.

Accessibility – Publication of business rule reports on a site developed and maintained by the business rules team ensures access at any time by anyone.

Reusability - Provides criteria to be used by development to further enhancements and write testing.

Accelerated time-to-market – Having a repository of business rules to reference for innovation and development gives users an understanding of the current state and provides a baseline for potential changes, in some cases decreasing the time to create project requirements by as much as 75 percent of the original time, and cost allotted. An industry professional estimated a project could save as much as 40 percent of the IT time and expense for a project by using the business rules and system architecture. By using these resources to understand the way the business and system are working today, a project no longer needs to begin by asking IT to mine the code for the same information. That time and budget could then be used for further innovation and enhancements.

4.2 Innovation

Use of business rules or decision approach or technology to solve business problems –Some real-life examples are:

- The actuarial department used business rules to determine hierarchies for operators and vehicles for certain rating decisions;
- The underwriting department corrected the application of a credit to capture information for all eligible parties;
- The defect management team uses rules for defect identification and resolution

Level of improved integration across business areas - Business rules help to improve a common understanding across business areas. An established vocabulary provides a common language that reduces confusion and improves communications across a wide variety of users. Incorporating business rules into a system architecture expands that understanding and integration even further.

Degree of support for complex business product or process configuration – Business rules are integral to creating a complete system architecture. Users can see where and when business rules come into play to impact processes, decisions and outcomes.

Improvement in customization or personalization – Based on customer feedback, we created a new kind of rule – the overview rule. The overview rule is the first rule in a group of rules and enables a quick understanding of the topic. Users also expressed a desire for simplification of more complex rules and meaningful ordering of rules within a report to improve comprehension.

Improvement in business agility – Business rules enable faster identification and correction of defects, ability to see where inconsistencies exist and address them, and facilitate deeper awareness and questioning of the current state. In addition, business rules are used to facilitate a common understanding for projects. For example, a project team started to change an underwriting plan and allotted two weeks for the team to research and understand the current plan and identify the changes that would be required. The Business Rules Management team provided the business rules along with an activity diagram, enabling the team to accomplish the task in two days instead of two weeks.

4.3 Impact and Implementation

At the time the P&C Business Rules Management team was created and charged with the responsibility of developing the business rules, the team didn't really know what a business rule was. One challenge quickly realized was that the term "business rule" is used in a variety of differing contexts and means something different to each user and audience. In addition to learning what a business rule truly is, education to users on just what is meant when the term "business rules" is used was needed. Over time, extensive researching and learning from the experts in the field, the team began sharpening their skills for writing rules, defining terms and developing concept models. It was fun! Other skills such as logic were enhanced and our business rule expertise can now be applied whenever the need arises.

Employees outside the Business Rules Management team have the advantage of spending less time on either end of the same activity. Previously it could take days, weeks or months to find necessary information, either as the party looking for a subject matter expert related to a specific topic or as the subject matter expert looking for the information being requested and responding to the request. A business rules repository makes the information available in one place, freeing up precious time for everyone.

The Enterprise Business Rules Management team was established a couple of years ago to help spread the word about the importance of business rules and provide assistance by helping teams document their business rules. Realizing the maturity level of the P&C Business Rules Management team over their experience, they often looked for our team's guidance and input regarding business rules, terms, concept models and the tool our company is using to build a business rules repository.

The journey was not without some issues to overcome.

Successful initiative to capture and express business rules, decision tables, terminology and concept models – It took us over two years to complete 100 percent of the policy and underwriting business rules. The team committed to the highest executive level to complete this journey and we were able to do so by the deadline set for us.

Significant scope and scale of the initiative's implementation (e.g. size, geography, value chain, organization, etc.) - It was easy to see that the task ahead was enormous. As of June 2018, the team has engineered and documented over 7,000 rules and continues working to keep them evergreen while adding more business rules focused on some reporting functions and billing. In addition, we have identified and defined a vocabulary of over 2,000 terms.

5. HURDLES OVERCOME

5.1 Management -

Obtaining executive sponsorships and getting buy-in was at times a challenge. You absolutely need support for your pilot and to help gain momentum to achieve success. The trick is to be able to sell your vision. You need to show the value and be upfront in explaining that it will not be immediate because it takes time to build a business rules repository, but in the long run the pay-off is more than worth the time and effort. The Business Rules Management team also had to take the time to explain what business rules are, how they are used and why documenting them is so important.

5.2 Business

The greatest hurdle related to our business partners was the pervading concern that this meant more work for them. For employees who are already at, or over capacity, this prospect makes it hard for them to get onboard. Again, the team took the time to explain the benefits and layout the approach, letting them know we would be doing the work and asking for their support and to provide some expertise when needed. Just like with management, it was imperative to take the time to explain what a business rule is, how it is used and why it is needed.

Organization Adoption – Spurring organization adoption takes work. Across the spectrum of audience that we spoke to, one of the primary things needing to be addressed was what is a business rule, what it does and why do we need them. As this is something we had to learn ourselves starting out, we knew that communicating this to our supporters and partners was key.

These days, everyone wants everything to be automated to help manage the workload. Many of our end-users wanted a way to connect the business rules to the system coding, so that if a change is made, the rules are automatically updated. Unfortunately, automatic updates were not an option for us. We had to assure our business and IT partners that we could maintain changes to the rules, even without automation, through a strong network of relationships and an awareness of the coming development projects being executed.

The team also encountered a challenge with some partners expecting all the business rules to be available to them immediately. It was necessary to set expectations, explain how much work it takes to complete an effort of the magnitude we were tackling and share with them the commitment we had made to leadership to complete them by the end of 2017.

Organization adoption of business rules takes a lot of hard work and strategy. Communication plays a huge role in organizational adoption. Everybody on the team must be a champion for business rules, making time to nurture and encourage others who are early adopters to take up the cause and spread the word.

Quality and consistency are also key. If you do not strive for the most current and accurate repository of business rules you can produce, a lack of maintenance and eventual obsolescence will cause users to abandon using the rules. In turn, causing you to lose the support necessary to continue growing your effort. Establishing a common format and identifying successful patterns and practices create clarity for users as they become more and more familiar with business rules.

Ask for feedback, often. Sincerely accept the good and the opportunities for improvement so that your users know how important they are to your team and its success. The end-user often sees what we do not as we sometimes get mired in the day-to-day tasks of our effort. Incorporate user feedback where it makes sense and where it is feasible. The easier it is to use business rules, the faster word will travel throughout the business will travel and help to expand your effort.

6. BENEFITS

6.1 Cost Savings / Time Reductions

Business rules provide the current state of the business at your fingertips. There is no longer a need to spend precious time, money and resources identifying the way the business is run today. This allows projects and development teams to produce requirements for changes to the current state faster than before. Cutting the time to deliver the necessary requirements significantly, speeding up development and delivering sooner on implementation.

6.2 Increased Revenues

Improving time to market leads to faster development and allows for quicker implementation than before. Increased revenues from early implementation can be realized sooner than anticipated. In addition, faster time to market also allows you to accomplish more than you otherwise would have, expanding the opportunities for innovation and development even further than before.

6.3 Quality Improvements

Having business rules fosters improvements in quality. Overall compliance is better because everything is documented and available to the end-user. Use of business rules in projects and development has the potential to reduce unnecessary mistakes or missed requirements that can result in defects, helping to reduce the number of defects experienced. For defects that do arise, the identification and resolution process is improved, reducing the time needed to identify an issue and providing immediate access to the criteria for the expected behavior so the resolution can be implemented faster than before.

7. BEST PRACTICES, LEARNING POINTS AND PITFALLS

7.1 Best Practices and Learning Points

- ✓ Learn from the experts
- ✓ Obtain executive support
- ✓ Talk to anyone that will listen
- ✓ Attend a conference
- ✓ Develop a guide for writing rules
- ✓ Use a specific method for writing rules
- ✓ Market your product
- ✓ Select a diverse team from seasoned employees with a variety of backgrounds, knowledge and expertise
- ✓ Get a good tool to help build your repository
- ✓ You're not going to get it right the first time – be flexible to change
- ✓ Celebrate milestones and successes along the way
- ✓ Be flexible and adjust as workloads and assignments change
- ✓ Obtain feedback from end-users regarding pain points and enhancements

7.2 Pitfalls

- ✗ Don't try to be too perfect starting out. Get something done, you can revise and refine later.
- ✗ Don't be timid to tell others about your successes. Shout it to the rooftops!
- ✗ Don't lose sight of the big picture and the end goal.

8. COMPETITIVE ADVANTAGES

In today's environment, if your company does not change, it will cease to exist. But change is not enough, it must be meaningful, and the speed of change is critical to be competitive. Business rules make that possible. Knowing what the rules are makes it easier to confidently adjust to change faster. The team just finished the initial effort at the end of 2017, so there's still work to do to move industry goal posts. The Business Rules Management team shares our story and vision unceasingly to anyone who will listen. Change can be difficult for people, even when it is positive. It takes time and effort to shift cultures and ways of thinking so that our partners embrace the benefits that business rules and system architecture provides them. A business rules repository in an agile environment enables the business to move more quickly furthering our competitive advantage. The business rules we have worked diligently to document, help to support our USAA mission and the strategic objectives our company is striving to achieve.

9. TECHNOLOGY

The team wanted to write business rules by business people using natural language. The Semantics for Business Vocabulary and Rules (SBVR) provides the standards and structure for this. The methodology we use is based on SBVR and is a set of guidelines for expressing business rules in a concise, consistent and clear business-friendly fashion. We use a tool for building our business rules repository that manages vocabulary, concept models, business rules, rule groups and reporting. The team leveraged a tool that manages and stores documents such as the business rules reports generated from our business rules repository tool for all users to utilize.

During our journey, the team learned many lessons, one was about the composition of a business rule. The methodology we use is very logical and we thought, by including every condition for every scenario related to the topic of the rule in one rule, that IT should love it. After all, this approach ensured that nothing would be missed or overlooked. However, what we found instead is that IT preferred the criteria be broken down into several smaller, logical rules and to trust that they would review all the rules that pertained to the topic. And, they were right – it is easier to read the rules and comprehend them quicker – and the business liked it too!

The big benefit of using the foregoing standards, methodology and tools is that business and technical people have a single source of the truth to utilize for their various needs. But we're not stopping there.

We've recently begun using a model-based system engineering tool that is taking this journey to a higher level and enhancing the overall understanding of how the business works. Using a tool to help model the business in its entirety is extremely beneficial. Especially one that can combine form, function and behaviour into one easy-to-understand illustration. The ability to incorporate the business rules within the depiction to indicate where they impact behaviour or decisions helps users to understand not only the significance of having your business rules documented, but also where the user may gain efficiencies, identify patterns, find opportunities and address potential gaps or issues. Documenting the business rules is a huge and important step. Seeing how the rules are integrated within and affect the business is imperative to successful strategic execution.

The journey shouldn't end with a business rule repository and a modelling approach. We must explore new technologies and innovations that can take our efforts to the next level. Is there a way to add traceability from the code to the source for business rules? Is there a way to automate some or all the updates made to them so that they stay evergreen with a minimum of effort freeing up to work on more complex issues with our business and IT partners?

10. THE TECHNOLOGY AND SERVICE PROVIDERS

SBVR™ – Semantics of Business Vocabulary and Rules – specifications published by the Object Management Group (OMG) regarding the use of structured natural language for a glossary of terms/definitions and business rules

https://www.omg.org/spec/SBVR/About-SBVR/

RuleXpress – a repository from RuleArts that manages terms, business rules, rule groups, concept models and decisions

http://www.rulearts.com/RuleXpress

RuleSpeak® - a proven set of guidelines for expressing business rules written by business people in concise, business-friendly fashion

http://www.rulespeak.com/en/

Consultants from Business Rule Solutions, LLC – provided excellent training and motivation. As we were further into the project, they provided an assessment of where we were and where we could improve.

http://www.brsolutions.com/

SharePoint – leveraged to develop a site to contain and manage the rule reports from RuleXpress. Keyword search functionality allows a user to search across all reports on the site.

https://products.office.com/en-us/sharepoint/collaboration

OPCAT – an open source tool for creating system architecture using Object-Process Methodology (OPM).

http://esml.iem.technion.ac.il/

Experts and Professors from MIT and the Technion - Israel Institute of Technology - provided guidance and encouragement as we continued to learn the discipline of Object-Process Methodology, as well as their support and troubleshooting expertise with OPCAT.

Building Business Capability conference – brings together other professionals you can learn from. Learn about the latest methodologies for success. Provides motivation and validation.

https://www.buildingbusinesscapability.com/

Section 3
Appendices

APPENDICES

Author Appendix

Layna Fischer

Publisher and CEO, Future Strategies Inc., USA

Ms Fischer is Editor-in-Chief and Publisher at Future Strategies Inc. She has also served concurrently as Executive Director of the Workflow Management Coalition (WfMC) and director of the Business Process Business Process Modeling Initiative (BPMI, now merged with OMG). She continues to work closely with these organizations to promote industry awareness of emerging technologies.

Future Strategies, Inc., (http://bpm-books.com) has published over 50 titles in print and digital editions within this industry sector including the annual *Workflow Handbook* series, a number of special editions and the annual *Excellence in Practice* series, profiling industry case studies and outstanding implementations.

Ms. Fischer has been involved in technology-related journalism and publishing for over 25 years.

In 2019, she received the coveted *Marvin L. Manheim Award for Significant Contributions to the Field of Workflow and BPM*.

Gladys Lam

Principal and Co-Founder of Business Rule Solutions, LLC

Gladys S.W. Lam is a world-renowned authority on applied business rule and decision techniques. She is Principal and Co-Founder of Business Rule Solutions, LLC (www.BRSolutions.com), the most recognized company world-wide in business rules and decision analysis. Ms. Lam is co-creator of IPSpeak™, the BRS methodology. She is Co-Founder of *BRCommunity.com*, a vertical community for professionals and home of *Business Rules Journal*. She co-authored *Building Business Solutions: Business Analysis with Business Rules*, with Ronald G. Ross, an IIBA® sponsored handbook on business analysis with business rules.

Ms. Lam is widely known for her lively, pragmatic style. Ms. Lam is an internationally recognized expert on business rules and decision techniques. She speaks internationally at conferences and other professional events. She co-presents interactive online seminars. She is also Executive Director of the *Building Business Capability (BBC) Conference*, which includes the *Business Rules Forum* and is the official conference of the IIBA®.

Ms. Lam is a world-renowned expert on business project management, having managed numerous projects that focus on the large-scale capture, analysis and management of business rules and decisions. She works comfortably with senior executives providing insights and advice. She advises senior management of large companies on organizational issues and on business solutions to business problems. She is most effective with mentoring and training business analysts worldwide.

Ms. Lam is most recognized for her ability to identify the source of business issues, and for her effectiveness in developing pragmatic approaches to resolve them. She has gained a world-class reputation for fostering positive professional relationships with principals and support staff in projects.

David Lyalin

Public Health Analyst, Centers for Disease Control and Prevention (CDC)

Dr David Lyalin is a recognized expert in analysis and improvement of public health operations and processes. He is a Public Health Analyst with the Centers for Disease Control and Prevention (CDC). Currently, Dr Lyalin concentrates on development and implementation of business rules solutions that capture operational best practices for Immunization Information Systems at CDC.

MARK NORTON

CEO & Founder, IDIOM Limited, New Zealand

Mark has spent four decades in enterprise scale software development, designing, using, and/proving model driven development approaches for customers world-wide in government, insurance/finance, health and logistics. In 2001, Mark established IDIOM Ltd. He has since guided the development program for the IDIOM decision management products and approaches to: simplify complexity; improve business agility; align business strategy and systems; and reduce development time, cost, and risk.

IDIOM is now focused on providing its customers with systems that foster and support nimble, continuous, and perpetual evolution of business best practice.

RONALD ROSS

Co-Founder & Principal, Business Rule Solutions, LLC

Ron Ross, Co-Founder and Principal of Business Rules Solutions, LLC, is internationally acknowledged as the "father of business rules." Recognizing early on the importance of independently managed business rules for business operations and architecture, he has pioneered innovative techniques and standards since the mid-1980s. He wrote the industry's first book on business rules in 1994. Ron is also the author of 10 professional books, as well as the executive editor of the Business Rules Journal. Through these publications, as well as on the online forum BRCommunity and his blog, Ron enjoys sharing his knowledge and experience in consulting and business rules.

KRISTEN SEER

Senior Business Rules Analyst, Business Rules Solutions, LLC

Kristen Seer is a Senior Consultant with Business Rule Solutions, LLC. She has worked as a business analyst in industries such as retail, pharmaceuticals, insurance, finance, energy and government.

Her practice focuses on helping clients introduce the business rules approach, including setting up centers of excellence, conducting training in the BRS Methodology™, mentoring business analysts, facilitating sessions to capture business rules, harvesting rules from source documents, redesigning business processes, and analyzing business decisions.

Her thirty-year career has encompassed roles as business analyst, rule analyst, data analyst, and project manager. Kristen is a regular speaker at the annual Building Business Capability conference (www.buildingbusinesscapability.com) and has written several articles published in the Business Rule Journal (www.brcommunity.com).

WARREN WILLIAMS

Branch Chief (retired), Centers for Disease Control and Prevention (CDC)

Mr. Williams previously served as the Branch Chief for the Immunization Information Systems Support Branch, National Center for Immunization and Respiratory Diseases, at CDC. He has been instrumental in the support, development and uses of business rules techniques in public health settings. Mr. Williams currently runs a land management firm.

Award-Winning Case Studies

Award	Nominated by:
Award California Bank	*Nominated by:* **Company:** OpenRules, Inc. **Website:** http://openrules.com
Award Deloitte Limited, New Zealand	*Nominated by:* Company: IDIOM Limited **Website:** www.idiomsoftware.com
Award IBM Global Sales Incentives	*Nominated by:* **Company:** IBM **Website:** www.ibm.com
Award IISSB at CDC	*Nominated by:* **Company:** IISSB **Website:** https://www.cdc.gov/vaccines/programs/iis/index.html
Award KPN, The Netherlands	*Nominated by:* **Company:** AuraPortal **Website:** https://www.auraportal.com
Award MMG Insurance, USA	*Nominated by:* **Company:** EA Department, MMG Insurance **Website:** http://www.mmgins.com
Award PowerHealth Solutions, Australia	*Nominated by:* **Company:** IDIOM Limited **Website:** www.idiomsoftware.com
Award Rabobank, The Netherlands	*Nominated by:* **Company:** Oracle **Website:** www.oracle.com
Award Traffic Control, Netherlands	*Nominated by:* **Company:** LibRT **Website:** https://www.librt.com
Award USAA	*Nominated by:* **Company:** USAA **Website:** http://usaa.com

INDEX

Reading and Resources
Get special 45% Discount on ALL these Books (see below)

BUSINESS RULES: MANAGEMENT AND EXECUTION

https://bpm-books.com/products/business-rules-management-and-execution

For corporate business readers who need to understand the meaning and impact of Business Rules in applications or scenarios such as why and how to use a rules-based approach to validate, transform, recalculate, and remediate complex applications; the art of managing rules and terminology in a consistent, business-friendly, and shareable way; how to use rules engine to achieve uniformity, consistency, continuous monitoring, transparency, flexibility, forecasting etc.

Key technologies, vendors and implementers in this ecosystem.

INTELLIGENT AUTOMATION

Rules, Relationships and Robots. Designing Strategies and Practical Implementation

https://bpm-books.com/products/intelligent-automation

Intelligent automation is about real business change and long-term value. If you're serious about transforming the nature of work in your organization through automation, you need to think beyond robotic process automation (RPA) and point solutions. A true intelligent automation strategy utilizes a combination of powerful technologies like AI, RPA, and data access alongside established processes to work holistically, resulting in smarter systems and actionable data insight.

DIGITAL TRANSFORMATION WITH BPM

"Today's BPM platforms deliver the ability to manage work while dynamically adapting the steps of a process according to an awareness and understanding of content, data, and business events that unfold," says Nathaniel Palmer. "This is the basis of intelligent automation, making BPM the ideal platform for digital transformation."

https://bpm-books.com/products/digital-transformation-with-bpm

INTELLIGENT ADAPTABILITY

As adaptive case management (ACM) systems mature, we are moving beyond simple systems that allow knowledge workers to define ad hoc processes, to creating more intelligent systems that support and guide them. Knowledge workers still need to dynamically add information, define activities and collaborate with others in order to get their work done, but those are now just the table stakes in a world of big data and intelligent agents. To drive innovation and maintain operational efficiencies, we need to augment case work—typically seen as relying primarily on human intelligence—with machine intelligence.

https://bpm-books.com/products/intelligent-adaptability

THRIVING ON ADAPTABILITY: BEST PRACTICES FOR KNOWLEDGE WORKERS

ACM helps organizations focus on improving or optimizing the line of interaction where our people and systems come into direct contact with customers. It's a whole different thing; a new way of doing business that enables organizations to literally become one living-breathing entity via collaboration and adaptive data-driven biological-like operating systems. --*Surendra Reddy*.

https://bpm-books.com/products/thriving-on-adaptability-digital

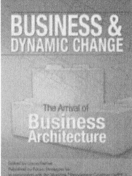

BUSINESS AND DYNAMIC CHANGE

The Arrival of Business Architecture

http://bpm-books.com/products/business-and-dynamic-change

These visionaries see the need for *business* leaders to define their organizations to be agile and robust in the face of external changes.

This book will stimulate thinking about a more complete approach to *business* architecture. As such, it is imperative reading for executives, managers, business analysts, and IT professionals that require an understanding of the structural relationships of the components of an enterprise.

BPM EVERYWHERE

Internet of Things, Process of Everything

http://bpm-books.com/products/bpm-everywhere-print

Critical issues currently face BPM adopters and practitioners, such as the key roles played by process mining uncovering engagement patterns and the need for process management platforms to coordinate interaction and control of smart devices.

BPME represents the strategy for leveraging, not simply surviving but fully exploiting the wave of disruption facing every business over the next 5 years and beyond.

PASSPORTS TO SUCCESS IN BPM:

Real-World Theory and Applications

https://bpm-books.com/products/passports-to-success-in-bpm

Is your BPM project set up for success or failure?
Knowing what BPM success will look like before you even begin will help you achieve it. So will knowing what are the most common causes of failure.
BPM projects fail more often as a result of missed expectations than inadequate technology.

EMPOWERING KNOWLEDGE WORKERS: NEW WAYS TO LEVERAGE CASE MANAGEMENT

https://bpm-books.com/products/empowering-knowledge-workers-print-edition

ACM allows work to follow the worker, providing cohesiveness of a single point of access. Case Management provides the long-term record of how work is done, as well as the guidance, rules, visibility and input that allow knowledge workers to be more productive. ACM is ultimately about allowing knowledge workers to work the way that they want to work and to provide them with the tools and information they need to do so effectively.

TAMING THE UNPREDICTABLE

https://bpm-books.com/products/taming-the-unpredictable-print-edition

The core element of Adaptive Case Management (ACM) is the support for real-time decision-making by knowledge workers.

Taming the Unpredictable presents the logical starting point for understanding how to take advantage of ACM. This book goes beyond talking about concepts, and delivers actionable advice for embarking on your own journey of ACM-driven transformation.

HOW KNOWLEDGE WORKERS GET THINGS DONE

https://bpm-books.com/products/how-knowledge-workers-get-things-done-print

How Knowledge Workers Get Things Done describes the work of managers, decision makers, executives, doctors, lawyers, campaign managers, emergency responders, strategist, and many others who have to think for a living.

These are people who figure out what needs to be done, at the same time that they do it, and there is a new approach to support this presents the logical starting point for understanding how to take advantage of ACM.

BPMN 2.0 Handbook SECOND EDITION

(see two-BPM book bundle offer on website: get BPMN Reference Guide Free)

http://futstrat.com/books/bpmnhandbook2.php

Updated and expanded with exciting new content!

Authored by members of WfMC, OMG and other key participants in the development of BPMN 2.0, the BPMN 2.0 Handbook brings together worldwide thought-leaders and experts in this space. Exclusive and unique contributions examine a variety of aspects that start with an introduction of what's new in BPMN 2.0, and look closely at interchange, analytics, conformance, optimization, simulation and more.

BPMN MODELING AND REFERENCE GUIDE

(see two-BPM book bundle offer on website: get BPMN Reference Guide Free)

http://www.futstrat.com/books/BPMN-Guide.php

Understanding and Using BPMN

How to develop rigorous yet understandable graphical representations of business processes.

Business Process Modeling Notation (BPMN) is a standard, graphical modeling representation for business processes. It provides an easy to use, flow-charting notation that is independent of the implementation environment.

See special 2-book offer online

iBPMS - INTELLIGENT BPM SYSTEMS

https://bpm-books.com/products/ibpms-intelligent-bpm-systems-print

"The need for Intelligent Business Operations (IBO) supported by intelligent processes is driving the need for a new convergence of process technologies lead by the iBPMS. The iBPMS changes the way processes help organizations keep up with business change," notes Gartner Emeritus Jim Sinur in his Foreword.

The co-authors of this important book describe various aspects and approaches of iBPMS with regard to impact and opportunity.

Social BPM

https://bpm-books.com/products/social-bpm-print-edition

Work, Planning, and Collaboration Under the Impact of Social Technology

Today we see the transformation of both the look and feel of BPM technologies along the lines of social media, as well as the increasing adoption of social tools and techniques democratizing process development and design. It is along these two trend lines; the evolution of system interfaces and the increased engagement of stakeholders in process improvement, that Social BPM has taken shape.

Get **special** 45% Discount on ALL Books

Use the discount code BOOK45 to get 45% discount on ALL books in the store; both Print and Digital Editions. Limit two copies per title.

Digital Edition Benefits:

Enjoy immediate download, live URLs, searchable text, graphics and charts in color. No shipping charges. Download from our website now.

Use this link to get 45% discount automatically applied at checkout:

https://bpm-books.com/discount/BOOK45

Published by Future Strategies Inc.
BPM-BOOKS.COM

Made in the USA
Monee, IL
26 May 2021

69518936R00103